Digital Dilemma

*Issues of Access, Cost, and Quality
in Media-Enhanced and Distance Education*

Gerald C. Van Dusen

*ASHE-ERIC Higher Education Report Volume 27, Number 5
Adrianna J. Kezar, Series Editor*

Prepared and published by

 JOSSEY-BASS
A Wiley Company
San Francisco

In cooperation with

*ERIC Clearinghouse on Higher Education
The George Washington University*
URL: *www.eriche.org*

*Association for the Study
of Higher Education*
URL: *http://www.tiger.coe.missouri.edu/~ashe*

*Graduate School of Education and Human Development
The George Washington University*
URL: *www.gwu.edu*

Digital Dilemma: Issues of Access, Cost, and Quality in Media-Enhanced and Distance Education
Gerald C. Van Dusen
ASHE-ERIC Higher Education Report Volume 27, Number 5
Adrianna J. Kezar, Series Editor

This publication was prepared partially with funding from the Office of Educational Research and Improvement, U.S. Department of Education, under contract no. ED-99-00-0036. The opinions expressed in this report do not necessarily reflect the positions or policies of OERI or the Department.

ISSN 0884-0040   ISBN 0-7879-5573-6

The ASHE-ERIC Higher Education Report is part of the Jossey-Bass Higher and Adult Education Series and is published eight times a year by Jossey-Bass, 350 Sansome Street, San Francisco, California 94104-1342.

For subscription information, see the Back Issue/ Subscription Order Form in the back of this journal.

Prospective authors are strongly encouraged to contact Adrianna Kezar, Director, ERIC Clearinghouse on Higher Education, at (202) 296-2597 ext. 14 or akezar@eric-he-edu.

Visit the Jossey-Bass Web site at www.josseybass.com.

Printed in the United States of America on acid-free recycled paper containing 100 percent recovered waste paper, of which at least 20 percent is postconsumer waste.

EXECUTIVE SUMMARY

Public discourse on the pedagogical uses of information technology runs the gamut of views from utopian to apocalyptic. A number of tacit alliances and formal partnerships between and among various ideologues have been forged with the objective of making shared views more credible to policymakers and institutional planners. Two ideologies in particular—both political constructs—have received much attention. The first, *restructuralism,* calls for radically restructuring postsecondary institutions from the ground up to respond effectively to social, demographic, and economic changes in society. The second, *incrementalism,* seeks evolutionary change as it preserves cherished principles of academic freedom, tenure, and faculty oversight. Both restructuralists and incrementalists share the conviction that institutions face "a triple challenge" of outcomes, accessibility, and costs (Ehrmann, 1995, p. 24). Although methods designed to achieve these ends will vary according to several factors, a foundation of common understanding based on research findings should center the debate and provide the basis for an acceptable resolution.

What Barriers to Higher Education Must Be Removed to Make Its Digitized Resources More Universally Accessible?

Leveraging technology to accommodate unprecedented growth and changing demographics requires overcoming a number of daunting obstacles to universal access. For colleges and universities, universal access operates on two levels: Intranet and Internet. Universal *Intranet* access refers to the ability of administrators, faculty, staff, and students to access campus networks for communication, instruction, research, scholarship, public service, and business processes and procedures. Major problems associated with universal Intranet access include (1) the inconsistent quality of off-campus dial-in networking services, (2) the shortcomings of campus computer labs, particularly as a critical safety net for on-campus students without computer access, and (3) the escalating costs of supporting an array of on- and off-campus software options and hardware configurations (Graves, 1997). Higher education providers will be hard-pressed to achieve the important goal of universal Intranet access without an unfaltering commitment to strategic and fiscal planning.

Universal *Internet* access refernology is often confused with its purchase price, but true costs are often staggeringly high—as much as ten times the purchase price when all expenditures are factored in, (4) assigning the actual cost to such intangibles as faculty course development requires new sets of economic tools, and (5) the adoption of student technology fees and computer requirements are often not well conceived or integrated into the strategic plan for campus computing (Ringle, 1997).

What Issues of Cost and Affordability Must Be Addressed to Ensure Universal Access?

Achieving the economies of scale made theoretically possible by technologically mediated instruction requires attention to a host of important issues: (1) institutional mission must be reviewed at the same time that a new vision of learning emerges, (2) intra- and interinstitutional collaboration must increase to ensure program articulation, delivery system integration, reduced duplication, maximization of limited resources, and preservation of underenrolled course offerings, (3) the cost of technology is often confused with its purchase price, but true costs are often staggeringly high—as much as ten times the purchase price when all expenditures are factored in, (4) assigning the actual cost to such intangibles as faculty course development requires new sets of economic tools, and (5) the adoption of student technology fees and computer requirements are often not well conceived or integrated into the strategic plan for campus computing (Ringle, 1997).

How Will American Higher Education's Reputation for Quality and Effectiveness Be Assured and Maintained in the New Technologically Mediated Environments?

Pedagogical issues in today's networked digital culture involve content, design, assessment, and support. Content problems arise from the Web's nonhierarchical structure and its increased commercialization (Burbules and Callister, 1998). The main design challenge facing faculty who move traditional courses to the Web or to interactive television is exploiting multimedia capabilities. Furthermore, such alternative forms of assessment—for example, authentic assessment and portfolio assessment—may prove to be more appropriate for students in technologically mediated environments. Finally, to assist faculty with integrating technology into instruction, institutions must commit to the provision of access to technology resources for faculty training, course design, and development; standardized configurations to ensure continuity between instructional paradigms and efficient technical support services; and appropriate consideration to the teaching function in tenure and promotion decisions.

What Conclusions and Recommendations Can Be Drawn?

In the current polarized political environment, quick, easy solutions to the challenge of making higher education more accessible, more affordable, and more effective are unlikely, although research findings do permit a number of specific conclusions:

1. Successful efforts to transform American colleges and universities are very likely to occur quite differently from institution to institution, based on institutional mandate, mission, and vision. Given the increasing number of adult and nontraditional students, it is likely that the majority of institutions will undergo some form of significant transformation.
2. Although in many respects colleges and universities are businesses, in crucial respects they are not.
3. The historic commitment to core values in traditional undergraduate education has wavered, and the same vacillation threatens to undermine general education requirements in electronically delivered certificate and degree programs.
4. Lack of Internet access results in information poverty for several classes of individuals and creates a new class of postsecondary institution.
5. Distance education is unlikely to effect institutional cost savings over the short or middle term.
6. Existing evidence on the effectiveness of media-enhanced and distance education is generally inadequate because of experimental design flaws.
7. Containing the costs of academic and administrative computing today requires a campuswide rather than department-level perspective.

The following seven recommendations address the pressing issues of access, cost, and quality:

1. Prepare to lobby more aggressively for state and federal policy reform of higher education issues.
2. Develop a reward system that places a high value on teaching and the innovative uses of technology, even though the two will be mutually exclusive in many cases.
3. Promote universal Intranet access to campus networks by standardizing hardware and software configurations.
4. Promote universal access to the National Information Infrastructure as a vital social utility.
5. Affirm the social nature of learning.
6. Require of all students the generic skills of mediacy and numeracy.
7. Preserve the quality and core values that undergird and distinguish higher education from corporate training, even as institutions work to untangle the knotty issues of productivity, efficiency, and effectiveness.

CONTENTS

FOREWORD

As distance education and virtual education options expand, most discussion of these topics centers on the positive aspects, such as low-cost, anytime-anywhere learning and the breaking down of discrimination, because virtual encounters mask knowledge of race or gender.

But a recent report by the College Board, "The Virtual University and Educational Opportunity," suggests a more ominous consequence of these new educational opportunities. They elaborate on a new set of barriers for the traditionally underrepresented in higher education, because computers are less likely to be in the schools and homes of low-income families. They note that "virtual space is infinite, but it does not promise universality or equity" (Gladiuex and Swail, 1999, p. 22).

Many are putting their hopes into Bill Gates's $1 billion program, which is attempting to ensure that all individuals have access to the Internet. But money alone will neither solve some of the problems nor capture the promise of this new technology.

What the College Board report and this monograph point out is that virtual and distance education, in addition to challenging our resources, faculty, administrative infrastructure, and student classroom experience, are also challenging our philosophy of education. The perennial philosophical questions once again emerge, such as who should be educated, what is the purpose of education, what are the social and political commitments to education, and what is a quality education.

Thus, we have been thrust into a time period of philosophical questioning in which challenging traditional assumptions is necessary. Too many people are running toward the new technology without asking some of these essential questions. Not Gerald Van Dusen. This monograph provides thoughtful questioning and forces a reexamination of core values.

Van Dusen, a second-time author for the series (his previous monograph was "The Virtual Classroom"), examines the promise (and some of the perils) of the new digital age. Van Dusen has years of experience with these issues, having worked in distance education at Wayne County Community College. As a faculty member, he is familiar with the applications of technology in the classroom and conducts research on alternative learning and instructional technology.

His combination of practical experience and research provides insight.

Van Dusen describes how cost and affordability issues need to be addressed to ensure universal access. Moving forward with virtual and distance education options as they are currently structured will result in a digital divide between those who have the skills and those who do not, and cost escalation will continue. Van Dusen examines processes for ensuring that quality and effectiveness will be maintained. His recommendations bring us back to the roots of higher education, reminding us that technology is likely to be integrated uniquely by each institution within this diverse U.S. system of higher education. He also suggests that distance education threatens general or liberal education and the value system undergirding it.

Van Dusen reminds us that higher education has distinctive purposes and values that it needs to maintain; those that advocate the change to a corporate, business, or entrepreneurial model are misguided, leading their followers down the wrong path.

There are several other ASHE-ERIC monographs that address similar issues. Faculty development and incentives are significant to integrating technology. "Successful Faculty Development and Evaluation," by John Murray, is a helpful resources on this issue. Of course, Gerald Van Dusen's earlier monograph, "The Virtual Campus," describes the steps to be followed to institutionalize technology on your campus. Also, Lion Gardiner's "Redesigning Higher Education" is an excellent summary of concerns related to student learning and ways to improve student outcomes. This monograph has a similar philosophical orientation and provides empirical evidence for the promotion of new teaching practices.

Adrianna J. Kezar
Series Editor
Director, ERIC Clearinghouse on Higher Education

INTRODUCTION

The greatest resistance to change will be found in those institutions whose traditional primary function has been the perpetuation of a society's folkways, mores, and values, such as religious and educational institutions. (Evans and Leppman, 1968, p. 31)

Public discourse on the pedagogical uses of information technology (IT) runs the gamut of views from utopian to apocalyptic. At the one extreme, IT is a magic bullet, an enabler of reforms that will silence higher education's critics by making the academy more accessible, more affordable, and more effective. Many technoutopians point particularly—and enthusiastically—to the major for-profit providers like the University of Phoenix, DeVry, and ITT, as well as to the avant-garde nonprofits such as Western Governors Open University and the Southern Regional Electronic Campus, as the new models for higher education.

At the other extreme, a coterie of skeptics warn of a brave new world of digital education, one in which students, recast as "customers," are "facilitated" rather than taught by legions of part-time and poorly paid instructors who depart from script at their own professional peril. Absent from this tableau, as Alan Wolfe sardonically notes in his assessment of the University of Phoenix, are "such accouterments of academic life as tenure, libraries, non-profit status, ivory-tower isolation, academic freedom, lectures, high tuition, the semester system, dormitories, beer bashes, full-time faculty members, *in loco parentis,* athletics, and the very idea of campus life" (1998, p. B4).

At the one extreme, information technology is a magic bullet, an enabler of reforms that will make the academy more accessible. At the other is a brave new world of digital education.

Historical Context

Almost completely lacking in an otherwise lively debate is the kind of historical perspective needed to temper the more excessive claims of either extreme. Calls for reform based upon the potential of alternative media have been heard before (Cuban, 1986; Saettler, 1968, 1990). Support for the integration of visual instructional materials into the curriculum, for instance, date back at least to 1928 with the publication of Anna Dorris's *Visual Instruction in the Public School* (Saettler, 1968). An audiovisual instruction movement flourished in the late 1940s, promoting a modern technological means of providing students with concrete or nonverbal learning experiences (Wagner, 1990). The weakness—and ultimate failure—of both reform movements was that they "emphasized materials at the expense of the instruction, and viewed the media as instructional aids rather than as an integral part of the instructional process" (Wagner, 1990, p. 13).

The 1950s saw significant economic commitment by the federal government and by a private foundation to the development of educational television. The National Defense Education Act (Title VII) of 1958, the Federal Communications Commission, and the Ford Foundation provided vital seed money for research and support of educational programming. When federal funding slowed, instructional use waned (Cuban, 1986).

Tyack and Cuban (1995) offer further instances of "pedagogical Nirvanas" that enthusiasts claimed would transform education, even replace teachers and produce superior student performance.

> *As new forms of pedagogy by machine appeared, a familiar cycle of reform recurred: hyperbolic claims about how a new invention would transform education; then research showing that the technology was generally no more effective than traditional instruction and sometimes less; and, finally, disappointment as reports come back from classrooms about the imperfections of the reform and as surveys showed that few teachers were using the tool.*
> *(pp. 121–122)*

Advocates of today's most advanced instructional technologies refute such generalizations by citing historical examples of their own. The printing press is just such an instance. Movable type, first introduced in the West by Gutenberg, fueled vast amounts of printing during the fifteenth century, supported the demands of late Renaissance scholars, and helped to spread the Reformation throughout Europe. Without Gutenberg's printing press, whose fundamental principles were not improved until well into the nineteenth century, the transition from elite to mass education might never have taken place.

So, too, technology enthusiasts contend, high-performance computing is transforming society, profoundly shaping how people work, shop, obtain and exchange information, and are educated. The ubiquity of powerful, affordable computing, coupled with the growth and development of the Internet and World Wide Web, comes precisely at a time when instructional technology theory is poised to transform practice. Contemporary systems models and concepts of instructional technology (Banathy, 1968; Dick and Carey, 1979) were developed to provide the framework for integrating what we have learned from behavioral science, cognitive psychology, and communications theory. Curriculum and course design have been revolutionized by systems thinking, which promotes the identification of the stages of the instructional design and development process. Systems thinking has produced significant activity in the areas of needs assessment, instructional sequencing, media production and use, and goal assessment (Wagner, 1990).

Acknowledging the inevitable problems and predicaments brought on by new technology, enthusiasts such as Rudenstine (1997) cite historical precedent for taking the long view. The problem today with the vast quantity—and mixed quality—of electronically transmitted information was foreshadowed centuries ago with the proliferation of books and the growth of libraries.

> *As early as the 18th century, Diderot looked upon the rapid proliferation of books and foresaw "a time . . . when it will be almost as difficult to learn anything from books as from the direct study of the whole of the universe."*
>
> *"The world of learning," he feared, "would be drowned in books." (p. A48)*

The proliferation of books and published materials continues to expand exponentially but within a system of classification and cataloging designed to promote access, systems that Diderot could not possibly have anticipated.

Studying the history of educational technology is particularly instructive in the present environment. Few technologies, we learn from history, achieve much success beyond modest experimentation. Fewer have staying power, and fewer yet revolutionize practice. A commentator describes one such new and significant innovation: "The inventor or introducer of this system deserves to be ranked among the best contributors to learning and science, if not among the greatest benefactors of mankind" (quoted in Tyack and Cuban, 1995, p. 121). The time was 1841, and the innovation was the blackboard. Are computers and Web-based management tools the new blackboards? Advocates of the new technologies say yes, resoundingly. The computer has become the "synthesis device" for a wide assortment of vital information and telecommunications technologies. Critics, on the other hand, warn that the new technologies, among other things, will drain precious resources long before the vaunted revolution occurs.

The Politics of Instructional Technology
This polarization of viewpoints about IT has taken a decidedly political turn. Although existing literature is replete with individual viewpoints, a number of tacit alliances and formal partnerships between and among various ideologues have been forged with the objective of making shared views more credible to policymakers and institutional planners. Two ideologies in particular—both political constructs—have surfaced atop the roiling sea of scholarly publication and conference presentations. The first ideology, *millennial restructuralism,* calls for radically restructuring postsecondary institutions from the ground up to respond effectively to social, demographic, and economic changes in society. The second ideology, *incremental reformism,* seeks evolutionary change even as it preserves cherished principles of academic freedom, tenure, and faculty oversight.

Millennial restructuralism
Millennial restructuralism is an ideology articulated primarily, but not exclusively, by members of a loosely based confederation of private foundations, trade associations, and academic-corporate consortia, such as EDUCOM and the American Council on Education; of edutainment and publishing companies, such as Disney and Simon and Schuster; of hardware and software vendors, such as IBM and Microsoft; and of community college and university administrators (Noble, 1998).

The rhetoric of restructuralism is founded on the doctrine of progress and its corollary, the doctrine of regress. The doctrine of progress, heavily influenced by an expanding market economy and a plethora of technological innovations to facilitate it, asserts that continued economic growth and a corresponding improvement in the human condition directly depend on the nature and quality of our educational system. To restore American economic hegemony, our schools and colleges must produce skilled knowledge workers able to function in a highly competitive, technologically intensive economic environment. Failure to "fix" an educational system perceived to be on the skids, according to the corollary doctrine of regress, will result in a devastating backward slide, socially and economically.

The idea of progress, originally a product of the European Enlightenment, had its earliest American manifestation in the writings and public pronouncements of Jefferson, Mann, and Webster, whose combined secular consciousness had a profound and lasting impact on the purpose and direction of education in American society. Public education for cultural progress, that is, education for both private virtue and public citizenship, has been gradually supplanted by the idea of public education for technological progress. According to a report from the National Association of Scholars, there has been, since 1914, a steady "purging from the curriculum of many of the required basic survey courses that used to familiarize students with the historical, cultural, political and scientific foundation of their society" (quoted in "College Has Lost," 1996, p. 2). For example, in 1914, 98 percent of America's leading colleges and universities had mandatory requirements for foreign language and English composition; by 1993, these numbers fell to 64 and 36 percent, respectively. Somewhat similar declines in mandatory requirements are noted for mathematics, history, and philosophy (*The Dissolution of General Education,* 1996). This trend and these numbers support David Hopper's contention (1991) that disillusionment from World War I and the emergence of science-based technology combined to shift the meaning and spirit of the idea of progress.

Millennial restructuralism acknowledges the values and espouses the intellectual foundation necessary for an informed citizenry. Its published literature, however, concerns itself mainly with addressing the threat to our nation's economy because of a severe shortage of technology-driven knowledge workers. Only by restructuring our community colleges and universities can we address this shortage and regain our economic hegemony.

To succeed in their reform agenda, restructuralists want to begin by overhauling key components of traditional academic institutions: the time and location of classes, the nature and methods of instruction, and the roles and responsibilities of faculty. As products of history—not some primordial creation—these key variables date as far back as thirteenth century France, with the establishment of the University of Paris. There, *le professeur,* the center of the academic universe, determined the time and place of study for students. In medieval Scotland, and later in colonial America, the credit-for-contact model was established. Students' progress became a function of hours clocked in the lecture hall, seminar room, or laboratory. Knowledge was relatively fixed, and the mastery of a discipline's content assured a stable career in a church- or state-sponsored occupation.

Over time, all parties have come to assume that these structural variables embody the necessary features of an authentic collegial experience. In fact, laws, institutional customs, and cultural beliefs have worked together to hold these structural variables in place for centuries. But variables—no matter their history—by definition are not immutable. And, at least according to the rhetoric of restructuralism, the time has come for radical change.

Under restructuring, time and place become fundamentally irrelevant as a precondition for teaching and learning. Until fairly recently, access to higher education for students constrained by time of class or distance from campus was generally limited to distance learning venues, such as correspondence study or telecourses. A number of newer technologies, however, including CD-ROMs, the World Wide Web, and interactive television, have begun to blur the distinction between media-enhanced, campus-based learning and distance education (Bates, 1996). The word *distance* becomes less relevant as a key descriptor for courses and students, James Hall contends, and alternative language must be applied:

> *Perhaps "connected" or "collateral" learning [would] be
> a more accurate descriptor. Collateral learning*

describes the growing availability of aids or alternatives that allow a student to review, speed up or substitute for some or all of what normally occurs in a classroom lecture. Such collateral options are becoming more commonly available, of higher quality, less costly to access, thereby of much greater importance to every institution. (1995, p. 5)

Restructuralists further contend that the opportunities for institutional leaders have never been greater to develop strategic plans appropriate to the ethos of their institutions that will foster the integration of these new technologies into the process of teaching and learning. But formidable obstacles remain. For instance, there are the twin tyrannies of what Robert Heterick calls "the tyranny of the classroom hour" (Hall, 1995, p. 6) and what J. C. Taylor calls "the tyranny of proximity" (1994, p. 179)—traditional mind-sets unwilling or unable to reform custom or practice. Within the public policy arena, Carol Twigg finds even more daunting obstacles:

We find regulations and funding formulas based on this paradigm of quality—e.g., FTE counts, contact hour definitions, financial aid requirements. Each of these policy positions reinforces the idea of credit for contact. The fact that distance education students are frequently ineligible for various kinds of federal and state financial aid is indicative of the problem. While alternatives to the credit-for-contact standard do exist, these outcomes-based standards need to become the rule rather than the exception. We need to create a better framework at the public policy level stimulating new approaches to instruction and for measuring institutional effectiveness. (1994c, p. 5)

A second key component of restructuralism, after the constraints of time and place have been removed, is a reconceptualization of teaching and learning for a knowledge-based economy. Advocates contend that a major change is taking place in the basic structure of the economy. The production, storage, and transfer of knowledge are the basis of wealth in the new economy. As Michael Hooker (1997) observes, "The trend in every sector of the economy is that the relative contribution of energy to the total value of the final product is declining and the relative contribution of knowledge is increasing" (p. 2). Because of tremendous advances in materials science, robotics, biotechnology, and telecommunications, production of our food, shelter, transportation, health, and recreation is accomplished with minimal manpower—a societal transformation. For example, in an energy-based economy, the mylar manufactured to produce a computer diskette becomes a product of economic value. In a knowledge-based economy, knowledge or information creates economic value, so although blank diskettes cost only pennies to produce and distribute, the information encoded on the diskette creates a final product worth hundreds or thousands times more than the transformed raw materials.

Knowledge workers in the new economy need to be able to find, filter, process, and disseminate information. The task is especially daunting when one considers the kind and quantity of information or raw data available daily to workers in memos, meetings, reports, phone calls, faxes, disciplinary journals, newsletters, and magazines, not to mention the expanding sea of Internet-based resources with their millions of websites, mailing lists, and usenet newsgroups, and many other protocols or resource types. Former Labor Secretary Robert Reich calls these workers "symbolic analysts," because their work most often involves "the manipulation of symbols—data, word, oral, and visual representations" (P. Robinson, 1997, p. 10). Their most valuable attribute, according to Reich, is the ability to "effectively and creatively *use* the knowledge" (p. 10). Traditional, behaviorally oriented pedagogy, with its emphasis on rote mastery of a discipline's content, must be replaced by a new, developmentally oriented "outcomes-based" pedagogy, one that emphasizes analytical and conceptual problem-solving skills and higher-level proficiencies in writing and reading along with effective individual and group communications skills. Such skills are critical components of lifelong learning. Because of the fluidity of technological change, those who prepare for a lifetime of learning, rather than content themselves with the receipt of a degree, will adapt better to social and economic change.

Revolutionary applications of information technology "have as yet to find complete expression in the structures and processes of any college" (Barr and Tagg, 1995, p. 15), but there is no dearth of imaginings in the literature of re-structuralism. A number of advocates, like Diana Oblinger, formerly of IBM, predict "the emergence of new structures made up of community colleges, private proprietary schools, corporate universities, school-to-work programs, and credentialed programs" (1998, p. 423). These new structures would define their market as continuous or lifelong learning and their "customers" as "employees first and traditional students second" (p. 423). In customized environments, students will be engaged in self-paced, independent study occurring anytime and anyplace and employing "learning materials that meet their own individual learning needs, abilities, preferences, and interests; they will learn how to learn" (Twigg, 1994b, p. 4).

The third key component of restructuralism would fulfill a trend more than a decade in the making: a reduction in the number and type of faculty. The American Council on Education reports that from 1987 to 1992, the proportion of part-time faculty and staff increased across all institutions, from 33 percent to 42 percent, while the proportion of tenured faculty declined, from 58 percent to 54 percent (*Straight Talk*, 1998, p. 14). Funding, available faculty in certain disciplines, and politics certainly have played a more important role than information technology during this transition to nontenured faculty. Nonetheless, these data represent a trend consistent with proposed new learner-centered environments in which a high degree of "faculty intervention" is neither necessary nor desirable; *disintermediation,* the word of choice, is the result of such a trend.

To be sure, the bulk of restructuralist literature emphasizes the changing roles and responsibilities of the instructional specialist in the new learning college. Among them are encouraging students to take greater responsibility for their own learning and engaging them in real- and hyper-world experiences that require the use of raw data and primary sources, along with manipulative, interactive, and physical materials. O'Banion (1996) prescribes an impressive list of responsibilities for those who aspire to be specialists: assessing learner abilities and needs, designing and creating learning options, selecting and repairing software, accessing and updating databases, establishing competencies and outcomes, and many others. Tenure and full-time status are not issues in the learning college, for specialists are independent contractors, delivering specified products or services for an agreed-upon fee. To emphasize the radical departure from past practices, O'Banion reminds us that *"wonderful teachers* and *great administrators* will be of no use in the learning college unless they can deliver special skills and abilities required by learners" (p. 23).

The cost-cutting implications of an increase in the proportion of part-time faculty and a reduction (elimination?) of tenured faculty are not lost on restructuralists. A former vice president of EDUCOM puts it into reductionist perspective:

> *Approximately 80% of the costs of colleges and universities are attributable to personnel costs; consequently, controlling costs means reducing the direct, personal intervention of faculty where possible in the teaching and learning process. The availability of a vast quantity of learning materials easily accessible via the network will make possible the creation of new kinds of learning environments. By lessening the need for direct faculty intervention in the learning process and increasing the ability of students to find and use learning materials on their own, we can create more cost effective instruction. (Twigg, 1994c, p. 3)*

Very little can be misinterpreted here: the sooner that sophisticated software can replace expensive—and soon to be redundant—faculty, the better for students and for institutional budgets.

Incremental reformism

Incremental reformism is an ideology articulated primarily, but not exclusively, by national faculty unions—the American Federation of Teachers, the National Education Association, and the American Association of University Professors—their state and local affiliates, discipline-specific associations such as the Community Colleges Humanities Association, the American Historical Association, the American Sociological Association, and the Modern Language Association, and many community college and university faculty and staff.

Because of a tendency by technoenthusiasts to label critics of instructional technology as backsliders or neo-Luddites, it is important to distinguish incremental reformers from individuals and groups representing the antitechnology movement. The latter movement may be characterized, at one extreme, as espousing a philosophy that advocates a rational alternative to the materialism and nihilism found in technologically driven societies. Davis's *technological humanism* is but one example of such an alternative. Schumacher and Norgaard offer alternative viewpoints. At the other extreme of the antitechnology movement are the *agrarian idealists* who, in some instances, argue for the complete eradication of technology in society (J. Robinson, 1997). None of the positions taken by these well-known proponents, however, ever reach the terrorist extremes we associate with the writings of Theodore Kaczinsky.

Incremental reformers, on the other hand, are neither antitechnologists nor political extremists. Academic scholars and classroom practitioners vary considerably in their attitude and in their use of communications and instructional technologies. For many members of this group, the new digital technologies represent additional tools with which to enhance existing practices, such as augmenting lectures and presentations, exploring supplementary sources of information and data, and increasing the venues for communication and interaction. According to the 1998 campus computing survey results, the majority of college and university faculty fall within this group (Green, 1998).

Many of the more reflective incremental reformers espouse the practice of *hybridization,* one in which classroom practitioners adapt reforms to classroom circumstances. In other words, the diversity of students and the uniqueness of learning communities call for the design and implementation of reforms by those holding first-hand perspectives, the teaching faculty. Tyack and Cuban (1995) have outlined the broad elements of such a model:

> *Under a hybridizing model of instructional reform—in which innovations are regarded as resources a teacher may adopt to improve instruction—a successful innovation may look quite different in practice . . . from classroom to classroom. In this approach, new*

curriculum frameworks, teaching methods, technology,
diagnostic tests, strategies for cooperative learning in
small groups, and other innovations are regarded not
as mandates from outsiders but as resources that teach-
ers can use, with help from each other and outsiders, to
help students learn better. (p. 138)

Faculty-based curriculum reform represents, according to critics of restructuralism, the antithesis of narrow and crassly economic and utilitarian motives for education. Atkinson-Grosjean (1998) forewarns that engaging in corporate-restructuralist thinking is intellectually dangerous: "It is antithetical to the questioning and skepticism we expect from those privileged to work in universities" (p. 2). But universities have become, or are rapidly becoming, consumer-oriented corporations led by administrators articulating a corporate discourse:

The adoption of corporate discourse on campus is one
facet of a persuasive new market-driven ethos [that]
commodifies the products of knowledge, and knowl-
edge itself, and offers them for sale in the marketplace
of ideas. Left unchecked, it valorizes application over
enquiry, research over teaching, and science and
technology over all other forms of knowledge. In doing
so, it neglects traditional areas of scholarship [that]
produce ideas rather than outcomes, and therefore
potentially undermines the university's wider social
role. (p. 2)

The university's "wider social role" of which Atkinson-Grosjean speaks has also been documented in a report entitled *Reaping the Benefits: Defining the Public and Private Values of Going to College* (Atkinson-Grosjean, 1998) prepared by the nonprofit Institute for Higher Education Policy. The study attempts to broaden the contemporary perception of college propagated by the media and policymakers—and assimilated by the general public—as a vehicle solely for employment and financial gain. In fact, the study finds both public and private social benefits accruing from a college education, benefits more extensive and significant than generally recognized. Public social benefits, for instance, include "reduced crime rates; higher voter participation (30% higher); more social cohesion and appreciation of diversity or social 'connectedness'; greater ability to adapt to technology; and more charitable giving and volunteerism" ("New National Report," 1998, p. 1). Private social benefits that were reported in the study include "longer life expectancy and better general health (increased exercise, less smoking, more leisure activities); improved quality of life for college graduates' children (higher cognitive levels and educational attainment); better consumer decision making; and improved personal status" (p. 1). To demonstrate balanced reporting, the study also presents the public and private economic benefits that accrue from a college education. Public economic benefits include "higher contribution to tax revenues; greater productivity (generating nearly all of the productivity increase within the last two decades); higher consumption; and reduced reliance on government financial support (Food Stamps, Medicaid, AFDC, etc." (p. 2). Private economic benefits reported are "higher lifetime and average salaries (some 73% more) for those who have gone to college; higher employment rates and greater job consistency; higher savings levels; improved working conditions and mobility" (p. 2). Institute President Merisotis notes that public dialogue on the value of a college degree has been restricted in recent years to one of economics: "The narrow focus on money and jobs as the primary outcomes of college distorts the broad value that we all derive from college education" (p. 2).

Critics of restructuralism express concern that, by focusing too narrowly on the practical aspects of finding work in a knowledge-based economy, we miss the forest for the trees:

> *The turbulence of contemporary change is best understood and dealt with against the background of history, literature, and those other timeless disciplines that connect us with the broader human experience. In a world of certificate-based education, we risk losing what may be of greatest value in traditional education. At risk is not just the quality of the lives of students whose education could be short-changed, but the ability of a democratic populous to make informed decisions. The Jeffersonian ideal of an educated democracy requires a breadth of education best provided by the classical liberal arts disciplines.* (Hooker, 1997, p. 11)

Therefore, the practice of hybridization reaffirms the centrality and the autonomy of individual faculty members in customizing learning environments to meet the broad needs of students. Integral to the success of hybridization, especially during periods of intense external pressure to reform educational practice, is the renewed emphasis on faculty oversight, the preservation of core academic values, and the insistence, as much as possible, on direct personal intervention. Critics of restructuralism contend that the use of new communication and instructional technologies should enhance and not diminish the value of these cherished principles.

Oversight, it is argued, can be effectively maintained only by a permanent faculty involved on a sustained basis through department and college governance mechanisms, such as committees that research market trends, develop new courses, establish requirements, design major, minor, and graduate programs, and oversee decisions about hiring, promotion, and tenure.

Recent trends in higher education, particularly the erosion of tenure and the increasing reliance on part-time faculty appointments, challenge the integrity of faculty oversight and threaten to undermine the quality of academic programs. Eight disciplinary organizations, the AAUP, and the Community Colleges Humanities Association have, in a joint statement, denounced this growing trend:

> *The immediate cost savings that institutions realize from widespread use of part-time appointments to staff introductory courses are often offset by the lack of program coherence and reduced faculty involvement with students and student learning. The frequently inadequate facilities accessible to part-time faculty members, coupled with the inadequate professional support they often receive, create structural impediments that put even the most talented teacher at a severe disadvantage. The limited time commitments of part-time employment mean that temporary faculty members do their work apart from the structures through which the curriculum, department and institution are sustained and renewed.* ("The Growing Caste System," 1998, p. 10)

Thus, an excessive reliance on poorly paid part-time appointments that offer no real career prospects, critics of restructuralism contend, can only discourage collegial involvement, classroom preparation, and curricular and professional development, and encourage a system of disparate personnel policies that inevitably engender cynicism and resentment.

The success of hybridization further depends on the preservation of academic freedom. Faculty theories, knowledge base, and research tools—already more developed and sophisticated than at any time previous—should not be allowed, it is argued, to become corrupted by outside pressure to promote such narrowly utilitarian agendas as restructuring is likely to produce. Academic careers already are "inherently vulnerable," as "producing knowledge or innovation often entails criticizing or rejecting conventional explanations or beliefs" (Allen, 1997, p. 75). Without the protection of tenure or some contractual arrangement providing such protection, reprisals from administrators, corporate sponsors, grantors, and other entities are more likely when ideas or studies undercut the assumptions underlying the investment. Robert Lynd, in *Knowledge for What* (1939), observed more than half a century ago that "radical research—in the sense of going to the root of the problem—may at times strike at the heart of a society's power system" (p. 27). In a restructured environment, with heavy corporate presence and participation, will the same free flow of ideas, particularly ideas that undercut the institution's power system, be tolerated as it has historically? Will adjunct faculty critical of the restructured environment be equally likely to be reappointed? Counterarguments that academic freedom is already protected by First Amendment guarantees, thus obviating the need for tenure or special contract language, simply do not square with case law and place on the dismissed or disciplined faculty member an unfair burden to litigate a constitutional right.

A third factor critical to the success of hybridization is the personal intervention of faculty in the learning experience of students. Although we expect students to achieve competence in applied skills and to master specific bodies of knowledge, we require more of a college-educated individual. According to Steven Crow, executive director of the North Central Association Commission on Institutions of Higher Education, we must go farther and define an educated person as "one capable of independent, critical thinking about the broader social, economic, cultural, and political environments in which all of us build our individual and corporate lives" (1997, p. 491). The development of critical-thinking skills, which are tools vital in both ideology frameworks, is a lifelong endeavor and entails the ongoing process of "conceptualizing, applying, analyzing, synthesizing, and/or evaluating information gathered from, or generated by, observation, experience, reflection, reasoning, or communication" ("Three Definitions," 1995, p. 2). Put another way, critical thinking is the "mental work involved when we investigate complex questions" (Kurfiss, 1989, p. 1). Questions are powerful motivators, and teachers can encourage students' responses and further inquiry by asking thoughtful, open-ended questions, which further encourage students to ask questions of themselves and of each other. Complex, thoughtful questions, which can have more than one response, challenge students to delve into issues more deeply and broadly and to form their own understanding of events and phenomena (Lunenburg, 1998).

Critical thinking is part of the dynamic relationship between how teachers teach and students learn. Most teachers, certainly great teachers, capitalize on "teachable moments" throughout the semester, moments when students' interest, knowledge, and enthusiasm intersect and transcend a particular lesson. A student's expression of interest—or lack of interest—however, does not, should not, determine whether a topic is taught or whether sections of the curriculum are eliminated. In the practice of hybridization, the faculty member steers students through the shoals of unprocessed data and misleading information.

A good example of what can happen when students are left to construct meaning on their own without faculty intervention is undergraduate research using the World Wide Web. Philosophy professor David Rothenberg (1997) has observed "a disturbing decline in both the quality of the writing and the originality of the thought expressed" when students use Web search engines "with their half-baked algorithms [that] are closer to slot machines than to library catalogues" (p. A44). The success students feel in finding hundreds, sometimes thousands, of supposed sources, often fragmented and superficial, reinforces the mistaken notion that research is easy. In a telling admission, Rothenberg concedes:

*But it's also my fault. I take much of the blame for the
decline in the quality of student research in my classes.
I need to teach students how to read, to take time with
language and ideas, to work through arguments, to
synthesize disparate sources to come up with original
thought. I need to help my students understand how to
assess sources to determine their credibility, as well as
to trust their own ideas more than snippets of thought
that materialize on a screen. The placelessness of the
Web leads to an ethereal randomness of thought. Gone
are the pathways of logic and passion, the sense of the
progress of an argument. Chance holds sway, and it
more often misses than hits. Judgment must be taught,
as well as the methods of exploration.* (1997, pp. A44)

Civilized man uses technology to expand inherent capabilities. If technology is essentially neutral, as many contend
and numerous studies purport to show (Clark, 1983; Russell,
1983), then new technologies in and of themselves are use-
less in promoting the values espoused by either mainstream
ideology. But both millennial restructuralists and incremental
reformers would agree that digital technologies have much
latent potential for teaching and learning. As Tony Bates,
director of distance education and technology at the
University of British Columbia, readily acknowledges, however, "The interaction between learner and a real teacher
can be substituted only to a certain extent by learning materials. Learners are always capable of generating questions
and ideas that cannot be adequately anticipated by machine-
based learning. If the learning system cannot handle this
diversity, then the quality of learning will drop" (1996, p. 4).

*Digital tech-
nologies
have much
latent poten-
tial for
teaching
and learn-
ing.*

Incremental reformers therefore take the position that
newer digital technologies offer the promise of a far greater
repertoire of teaching and learning strategies, of increased
access to higher education for students constrained by time
and location of class, and of acquisition of new skills necessary for employment in the information age. Reformers further acknowledge the tremendous potential of new and
emerging software applications, virtual labs, and expert
systems to enhance higher-order cognitive skills. What is
lacking at the moment, however, is any "convincing or systematic research evidence to suggest that students are actually acquiring and using these skills, or that this is the best

way to get to those outcomes" (Bates, 1996, p. 8). In the meantime, there is both a philosophical and economic basis for an institutional approach that Collins and Berge (1994) call *technological minimalism,* "the unapologetic use of minimum levels of technology, carefully chosen with precise attention to their advantages and limitations, in support of well-defined instructional objectives" (p. 8). Whenever programs and courses go beyond traditional delivery technologies—blackboard and chalk, for instance—issues of access, cost, and quality become immediate and serious. The best people to consult on these issues, within the framework of fiscal and strategic planning, are those most intimately involved in the teaching and learning process—the faculty.

Implications for Colleges and Universities

At one time, members of academic institutions may have viewed themselves and their organizations as apolitical, somehow outside the pale of society's factional intrigue and immune to the influences of unscrupulous partisans. This was, of course, never quite the case, but certainly "in the last hundred years colleges and universities have become integral parts of the society they serve" (Curry, 1992, p. 22, quoting Martin Brubacher). For lasting change—incremental or structural—to occur within these institutions, advocates must act *politically* by discerning individuals' and groups' motivations for supporting or resisting change and by mobilizing human and material resources to influence or persuade members about the merits of the change.

In politically charged environments, the most potent weapons are not always facts and closely reasoned arguments. Too often power begets aggression and decisions are based on narrow interests and agendas. In areas of shared conviction, however, research findings can shed light, and they provide a useful framework for developing pathways of least resistance to common goals. Both millennial restructuralists and incremental reformers share a common conviction that most institutions are facing what Ehrmann (1995) terms the "Triple Challenge of outcomes, accessibility, and costs. If not now, then in the next few years they will find it increasingly difficult to offer a modern, effective academic program that reaches and retains the students they should be serving for a price that those students and their benefactors can afford. For many institutions, these three issues of outcomes, accessibility, and costs pose real threats to their reputation and [well-being]" (p. 24). Although methods designed to achieve these ends vary according to several factors, a foundation of common understanding based on research findings should center the debate and provide the basis for a resolution acceptable to all constituents.

Organization of This Report

The focus of this monograph is of necessity limited to a discussion of the three major goals of reform: access, cost, and quality. The next section takes up issues of access and equity. Institutions attempting to leverage technology to accommodate unprecedented growth face a number of daunting obstacles in the path of universal access. The specific barriers discussed are age, income, race and ethnicity, gender, previous education, geography, household type, physical disabilities, and learning disabilities.

The third section, "Issues of Cost and Affordability," examines a range of issues that must be addressed if the economic benefits of technologically mediated instruction are to be achieved. The issues include institutional mission and vision, efforts at collaboration and cooperation, price versus cost of technology, tangible versus intangible costs, and student technology fees and computer leasing arrangements as partial solutions to the fiscal dilemma.

The fourth section, "Issues of Quality and Effectiveness," reviews a range of pedagogical issues linked to media-enhanced and distance learning and not typically encountered in the traditional classroom. The specific issues include the problem of Internet content, instructional design considerations, on-line assessment, and institutional support of faculty who integrate technology into instruction.

The final section draws seven conclusions from the literature and makes seven recommendations for policymaking and institutional planning.

ISSUES OF ACCESS AND EQUITY

The test of progress is not whether we add more to the abundance of those who have much; it is whether we provide enough for those who have little.
—Franklin Delano Roosevelt (1937)

Since World War II, access to higher education in the United States has expanded rapidly. In the immediate postwar period, nearly one-third of the relevant age cohort, 18–22, was enrolled in postsecondary institutions. By the 1960s, this proportion had increased to approximately 50 percent, the highest proportion among the industrialized nations of the world (Altbach, 1992). This dramatic transition from elite to mass education was accompanied by an equally dramatic expansion of physical facilities—particularly new classrooms, laboratories, libraries, and residence halls—to accommodate the enormous influx of students.

To broaden access and sustain growth, different types of providers, from the burgeoning public two-year "community" colleges to some of the most prestigious and expensive private universities in America, began to experiment with nontraditional venues, such as night and weekend classes, extension campuses, and distance education. Over time, however, the costs of expanded access and sustained growth were so staggering that many institutions faced the very real prospect of insolvency. Today, deferred maintenance costs nationwide for an aging campus infrastructure surpass $26 billion (*Straight Talk,* 1998). In many instances, expansion of existing facilities is not considered economically feasible, yet the two obvious alternatives—to further strain physical facilities by crowding classrooms beyond their intended capacity and to curtail access—are equally untenable. Both options would undermine educational quality and reverse three decades of public policy designed to expand college opportunity (Finney, 1997).

Universal Access

In recent years, encouraging developments in digital communications technology, particularly in Web-based environments, have renewed hopes that expanded access to higher education can be achieved without sacrificing educational quality or courting financial disaster. Both reformers and restructuralists would agree that, properly designed, new and emerging technologies will open access to populations

Properly designed, new and emerging technologies will open access to populations that have enjoyed only peripheral participation in higher education.

that have enjoyed only peripheral participation in higher education. Such "universal access," as it has been called, would fulfill the democratic progression, in Martin Trow's phrasing, from elite to mass to universal higher education (Altbach, 1992).

Access to what?

Historically, *universal access* (known also as *universal service)* has meant bringing basic telephone service to outlying rural areas at reasonable cost. Over time, the meaning has evolved to include emergency 911 and operator-assisted service as "a vital social utility that should be available to all citizens" (Clement and Shade, 1996, p. 1). Only recently has universal access been identified as a goal intended to mitigate the disparities between the information haves and the have-nots. To be effective, access to this new information infrastructure must be redefined as "not only establishing physical connections to the network, but also insuring that those connections are easy to use, affordable, and provide access to a minimum set of informative resources. In particular, network use should not be limited to the passive receipt of information. Instead, the environment should be open, distributed, and easily navigable. Even the most basic connection should enable users to act as information sources as well as destinations" (Keller, 1995, pp. 34–35).

Today, the concept of *information* transcends its traditional denotation: knowledge derived from study, experience, or instruction. Digital technology expands the concept by fusing information with communication to such an extent that "we cannot define where one ends and the other begins" (Coyle, 1995, p. 2). In 1994, the Clinton administration appointed the Information Infrastructure Task Force to develop strategies to more fully exploit the increased bandwidth and high-speed connections made possible by new advances in telecommunications technology. The goal was to make digitized information resources universally available to the entire Internet community—the supercomputing centers, the scientific and research community, the K–12 and higher education community, libraries, hospitals, businesses, industries, and the general public. The project, dubbed the National Information Infrastructure (NII), would work to encourage the commercial development of the information infrastructure by eliminating regulatory barriers.

An information infrastructure has already been in place for a number of years. For example, radio, telephone, and television transmission, audio and video cassette recordings, CD-ROM, computers, and fax machines have offered unprecedented levels of information and communication for several years. NII seeks to expand and integrate this infrastructure by way of a high-speed, digitized, interactive broadband network. The emerging digital communications system has tremendous potential to support our traditional, distributed, and continuing educational system, to conduct research and disseminate scholarly information, to increase democratic participation in local, state, and federal government, to improve the nation's health care system, to make available the rich cultural resources from around the world, and to spur economic growth through a variety of commercial endeavors ("The Administration's Agenda," 1993).

Higher education and NII

Within the higher education community, the relevant components of NII must be understood less as a campus-based resource and more as a vital public sphere. The evolving technologies that will fuel many forms of formal higher education will be the same ones providing access for continuing education, for civic participation, and for future employment. Anderson and Bikson (1998) contend that "most Americans will have to become Internet literate in the near future just to carry out the day-to-day activities of citizens in a developed society, quite independently of the computer skill demands made on them by their workplace" (p. 1). Knowledge workers require—and active citizens depend on—an information infrastructure that is at once equitable, affordable, and ubiquitous.

Institutions attempting to leverage technology to accommodate unprecedented growth and changing demographics face a number of daunting obstacles in the path to universal access. For colleges and universities, universal access operates on two levels: Intranet and Internet. Universal *Intranet* access refers to the ability of administrators, faculty, staff, and students to access campus networks for the purpose of instruction, communication, research, scholarship, public service, and day-to-day academic and business processes and procedures. Intranet access has five components:

- Connections *between campus buildings—the fiber network inter-connecting all buildings on the contiguous campus, including any residence halls;*
- Connections *from the campus network to off-campus programs—whether housed in institutionally owned or leased space;*
- Connections *within building—wiring infrastructure and network electronics within each institutionally occupied building, including any residence halls;*
- *Mobile* connections *to the campus network by individuals—from home or when traveling or conducting field work, for example;*
- *Personal and convenient* access *to a computer—one that is, or easily can be, attached to the network for studying or conducting business.* (Graves, 1997, p. 50)

Major problems associated with universal Intranet access include the inconsistent quality of off-campus dial-in networking services; the shortcomings of campus computer labs, particularly as they constitute a critical safety net for on-campus students without computer access; and the escalating costs of supporting an array of on- and off-campus software options and hardware configurations. Higher education providers will be hard pressed to achieve the important goal of universal Intranet access without an unfaltering commitment to strategic and fiscal planning.

Universal *Internet* access refers to the ability of society at large to access the National Information Infrastructure, which of course includes a significant educational component. According to the Department of Commerce (1995, 1998, 1999) and the College Board (Gladieux and Swail, 1999), a persisting "digital divide" exists among various income levels, demographic groups, and geographic areas. Although Americans have increasingly embraced digital technologies, a number of specific roadblocks along the information highway must be averted. Specific barriers include age, income, race and ethnicity, gender, previous education, geography, household type, physical disabilities, and learning disabilities. These barriers cannot be ignored, for the individuals within these groups now represent, in aggregate, a majority of the present and projected student population.

Age

Today more than 14 million Americans attend public and private colleges and universities (National Center for Education Statistics, 1997). The fastest-growing segment of the college market is adult students—those students 25 years of age and older—who make up nearly half of all college enrollments in this country. Fewer than one quarter, or about 3 million students, attend full time and are under 23 years of age. Furthermore, more full-time students are forsaking dormitories to live on their own off campus. Thus, traditional students are no longer the norm on our nation's college campuses.

Universal access for nontraditional students means not only technical access but also access to technology-based learning opportunities adapted to their special needs. Moreover, the educational needs of nontraditional students cannot always be met in traditional ways. Ninety percent of adults who return to school do so to change or advance in their careers. Seventy percent seek degrees and want to complete their educational objectives quickly and efficiently (Aslanian, 1998). Colleges and universities have responded to the special needs of adult learners with alternative delivery options such as accelerated degree programs, flexible scheduling, off-campus sites, shorter courses, and weekend college. Adult learners also need quick and convenient access to NII, however, either to satisfy campus course requirements or to pursue on-line courses or degree programs.

Data from three Commerce Department reports, *Falling Through the Net* (1995), *Falling Through the Net II* (1998), and *Falling Through the Net: Defining the Digital Divide* (1999), as well as a meticulous analysis by the College Board, *The Virtual University and Educational Opportunity* (Gladieux and Swail, 1999), show a consistent pattern of uneven access to NII based on age. (The complete reports, including charts and graphs, are available at http://www.ntia.doc.gov/ntiahome/fallingthru.html, http://www.ntia.doc.gov/ntiahome/net2/falling.html, http://www.ntia.doc.gov/ntiahome/fttn99, and http://www.collegeboard.org.) Universal access to NII

Universal access for nontraditional students means not only technical access but also access to technology-based learning opportunities adapted to their special needs.

assumes nearby, convenient, and affordable devices that people can operate, such as telephones, PCs, and modems. According to the most recent data, the youngest age group (under 25 years) has the lowest rate for telephone penetration at 87.6 percent. Seniors (55 years and older), on the other hand, have the highest telephone penetration rate at 95.6 percent. With respect to computer and modem penetration, seniors had the lowest rate at 25.8 and 14.6 percent, respectively, followed by the youngest age group with 32.3 and 20.5 percent, respectively (Department of Commerce, 1999).

Although the youngest age group has the lowest telephone penetration rate and the second-lowest computer and modem penetration rates, traditional students make up a significant portion of this group and have greater campus access to these technologies in residence halls, classrooms, and laboratories. However, one trend is worth monitoring: more full-time students are forsaking dormitories to live on their own off campus. During the five-year period 1992–1997, the number of undergraduates living off campus increased from 80 percent to 85 percent (Dubois, 1997).

A growing number of older adult learners (55 years and older) need to become adept at the new digital technologies for informal and lifelong learning, mental stimulation, personal enrichment, and, perhaps most important, vested membership in an increasingly electronic global community and economy. For seniors, going on-line means acquiring information on books, travel, and genealogy, sharing knowledge and experience in focused discussion groups, and keeping in touch with family and friends by way of electronic mail (King, 1997). A number of physical and psychological obstacles, however, restrict access to the new media. Nearly half of older adults by the age of 65 have a disability related to mobility, agility, vision, hearing, or speech (Rowlandson, 1997). The new technologies must be adapted and adaptable to seniors' special physical needs. For example, "screen magnification" software is available to provide higher levels of magnification and additional color and contrast enhancement (Access Technology, 1998). Furthermore, many older learners express anxiety over the rapid pace of change generally and the proliferation of new technologies specifically. Psychological difficulties can be mitigated to some degree by a structured program of learning that addresses key issues such as appropriate physical environment, program design, program delivery, and evaluation (Arsenault, 1997). Crucial to many older learners' psychological well-being, for example, is a less stressful physical environment, one that is safe, quiet, and well lit, and one with ergonomically designed seating and appropriately modified technologies (Arsenault, 1997). These preconditions are not only reasonable but essential for universal access to today's technologies for older adult learners.

Income

Perhaps the most reliable determinant in distinguishing between the information haves and have-nots is income. Telephone, computer, and on-line access remains markedly a function of household earnings. The poor—more often found in rural areas and central cities—lag significantly behind the middle class and the affluent in access to NII.

This gap between the information rich and the information poor appears to cut across the middle of the U.S. population and should be understood within the broader context of national income distribution. In a study of American living standards, Rand Corporation labor economist Lynn Karoly found that from 1989 to 1993 inflation outpaced gains in income for one-half the population ("Rand Corp. Study," 1996, p. 1). Most disturbing is the worsening living standard for millions of Americans, particularly for single-parent families. By contrast, those who advanced economically were generally older, well educated, and from families led by married couples. Karoly ironically concludes, "We might have been willing to live with more inequality if everyone was better off, but that's not the case" (p. 1). The Rand Corporation's findings represent an update on the widely reported national trends of growing economic inequality in the 1970s and 1980s.

More particularly, telephone, computer, and modem penetration generally match the pattern of income distribution. Households earning less than $20,000 per year lag behind the national average for telephone penetration; those with incomes below $35,000 trail the national average for computer and on-line access (36.6 percent and 26.3 percent, respectively). By contrast, households with incomes above $75,000 had computer and on-line access rates of 79.9 percent and 62.0 percent, respectively (Department of

Commerce, 1999). What is most significant about the data is that the gap in computer and modem access levels between higher-income and lower-income households actually widened by nearly 10 percent during the three years between the original Commerce Department study in 1994 and the follow-up study in 1997.

In Canada, similar results have been obtained. For instance, Frank (1995) reports findings of a Statistics Canada study correlating household income with computer and modem access. By 1994, households in the highest reported income range were five times more likely to have computers at home (46 percent) than were those in the lowest income range (9 percent).

If intelligent applications of IT have the power to transform the national economy and the communities where we live, then according to Anne Beamish (1996), we must be concerned with answering two fundamental questions: "First, what impacts—social, economic, political and spatial—are advanced technologies likely to have on cities, especially on low-income communities? [Second,] how can we capture the benefits of the new technology and at the same time avoid its possible negative effects— the creation of informational 'haves' and 'have-nots,' the weakening of communities of place, the uses of the technology for purposes of coercion and control?" (pp. 1–2).

Unfortunately, the outlines of a two-tiered society have already taken shape, for all the data presently available remain remarkably consistent. In *High Technology and Low-Income Communities* (Schon, Sanyal, and Mitchell, 1998), several contributors propose five initiatives for using IT to benefit low-income communities:

- *To provide access to the new technologies in ways that enable low-income people to become active producers rather than passive users;*
- *To use the new technologies to improve the dialogue between public agencies and low-income neighborhoods;*
- *To help low-income youth to exploit the entrepreneurial potential of information technologies;*
- *To develop approaches to education that take advantage of the educational capabilities of the computer;*

- *To promote the community computer: applications of computers and communications technology that foster community development.* (iii)

The prospects for success with these initiatives, however, will be far less likely to occur without considerable influence exerted on federal, state, and municipal policymakers.

Race and Ethnicity
The relationship between race and ethnicity and information access remains unsettled because of conflicting data from various sources. The most comprehensive studies, however—Novak and Hoffman (1998) and the Department of Commerce (1995, 1998, 1999)—are fairly consistent within certain select parameters.

Novak and Hoffman base their analysis on primary data obtained from the spring 1997 CommerceNet/Nielsen Internet demographic study. This particular national study was the first to correlate data on Internet use by race and ethnicity. Novak and Hoffman conclude that whites are significantly more likely than blacks to own a home computer (44.2 percent versus 29 percent), to have ever used the World Wide Web (26 percent versus 22 percent), to have used the Web at home, at work, and at other locations other than at school (22 percent versus 15 percent). But at other points in the study, results are ambiguous. For instance, for household incomes above $40,000, race is no factor in predicting home computer ownership, yet in the case of students, whites more frequently than blacks own computers even when the data are statistically adjusted for students' household income.

The three Commerce Department reports on access to information services (1995, 1998, 1999) reveal similar patterns. The data from all three years show a significant divide among racial and ethnic groups for telephone penetration, computer ownership, and on-line access. Rates for telephone penetration are highest for white households (95.9 percent), followed by "other non-Hispanic," which includes Native Americans, Asian Americans, and Eskimos (76.4 percent), Hispanics (84.6 percent), and blacks (85.4 percent). The information access gap is even more pronounced for computer ownership and on-line access.

Whites (46.6 percent) are twice as likely as blacks (23.2 percent) or Hispanics (25.5 percent) to own a computer. Unlike in the Novak and Hoffman study, the gap in computer ownership between whites and blacks continues at all income levels, even above $75,000. At the same time, on-line access rates for whites (29.8 percent) are nearly three times those for blacks (11.2 percent) and Hispanics (12.6 percent). The most disturbing finding in the Commerce Department studies is that the gap in computer ownership among the races actually increased between 1994 and 1997. For instance, between white and black households, the computer ownership gap increased by 4.7 percent; between whites and Hispanics, by 6.6 percent.

> **In one four-year period, the digital divide became a "racial ravine."**

Most troubling about the Commerce Department data is how, in one four-year period, the digital divide has become a "racial ravine." Between 1994 and 1998, the computer ownership gap between white and black households increased 39.2 percent (from a 16.8-point gap to a 23.4-point gap). During the same period, the gap between white and Hispanic computer ownership increased 42.6 percent (from a 14.8-point gap to a 21.1-point gap). The ravine deepens when Internet access is considered. Between 1997 and 1998, the gap in modem penetration between whites and blacks grew 53.3 percent (from a 13.5-point gap to a 20-point gap). Between white and Hispanic households, the gap grew 56 percent (from a 12.5-point gap to a 19.5 point gap).

Wight (1997) reports on two studies that challenge the findings of Novak and Hoffman and of the Commerce Department. The first, a survey by Lou Harris and Baruch College published in the April/May issue of *Public Perspective,* finds that Internet users are made up of "almost equal percentages of whites (30 percent), African Americans (27 percent) and Hispanics (26 percent)" (p. 1). The second, a study conducted by and reported in the May 1997 *Target Market News,* a newsmonthly of black consumer marketing, asserts that "African American households have traditionally spent more than whites on such items as apparel, food and telephone services. The latest item to be added to this list is access to the Internet. Compared with white households, blacks spent 2.5 times more for on-line services" (p. 2).

Presently, more raw data and information about the impact of low-end (under $1,000) personal computers, aggressive public wiring programs, and Web TV have to be accumulated before a clear snapshot of the digital divide can be taken.

Gender

The participation of females in postsecondary education has advanced incrementally ever since such statistics were first tabulated following the Civil War. In the 1869–70 academic year, for example, undergraduate enrollment for men outpaced enrollment for women 4 to 1, or 41,160 men to 11,126 women (*Digest,* 1997, Table 171). By the turn of the century, the ratio had improved to 5 to 3, or 152,254 men to 85,338 women (Table 171). Statistical parity was eventually achieved in 1978, when half of the total U. S. undergraduate enrollment of 11.2 million were women (Table 172). In the most recent year tabulated by the *Digest for Education Statistics* (1997), total 1995 fall enrollment for women surpassed that of men by nearly 4 to 3, or 7.9 million women to 6.3 million men (Table 175). A large part of this remarkable transition can be attributed to the influx of adult students, 65 percent of whom are women (Aslanian, 1998).

Notwithstanding the numerical parity achieved in enrollment statistics, women remain marginalized in such academic disciplines as computer science and engineering (Hill, 1997), in the IT workplace (Gladis, 1998), and in access to NII (CommerceNet, 1998). Though they earn 50 percent of all bachelor's degrees awarded, relatively few women pursue degrees in computer science (22 percent) or computer and electrical engineering (13 percent) (ITAA Report, 1998).

Women represent 41 percent of the IT workforce, which appears reasonable given the low percentage of technical degrees earned. When low-end IT jobs such as data entry specialists and computer operators are discounted, however, women represent only 25 percent of the remaining professional positions (Information Technology Association of America, 1998). Especially disconcerting is that although 35.8 percent of all undergraduate and graduate computer science degrees were awarded to women in 1984, by 1996 the percentage had declined to 28.4 percent (Gladis, 1998), suggesting that female representation in the IT workforce is likely to get worse before it gets better.

Several recent studies reveal a gender gap in access to NII. The CommerceNet/Nielsen Internet demographic survey indicates that women represent 43 percent of Internet users (June, 1998). A World Wide Web user survey conducted by Georgia Tech University shows disproportionate use of the Web by males (82 percent), but, compared to an earlier survey, female representation increased by 6 percent (Graphics, Visualization, and Usability Center, 1995). In one study conducted by Matrix Information and Directory Services and Texas Internet Consulting, gender parity appears to be greater at postsecondary institutions. The authors report Internet use by women at colleges and universities of 41 percent, compared with 30 percent at other types of organizations (Quarterman and Smoot, 1995).

Technology holds enormous potential for equalizing access to information resources for marginalized groups such as women.

Technology holds enormous potential for equalizing access to information resources for marginalized groups such as women. Digital technologies are still in their infancy, and compensatory pedagogical adjustments must be made, some scholars contend, to mitigate the disadvantages women have faced "from childhood through post-secondary educational experiences, and at work in a technology-dominated culture" (Campbell, 1997, p. 6). Feminist scholar Bonnell and others claim that "women's learning styles differ from men's, and that women react better than men to certain teaching approaches (Blumenstyk, 1997, p. A36). Ever since the publication of *Women's Ways of Knowing* (Belenky and others, 1986), challenging as it did a number of traditional epistemological assumptions, adult learning theorists have attempted to differentiate pathways to knowledge that typify one gender or another. Media-enhanced and distance education have become fertile areas around which to test hypotheses and reinvigorate the debate.

Previous Education
Still another variable that fairly accurately predicts one's level of access to NII is educational background. High household income, as we have seen, positively influences computer ownership and on-line access to NII; however, Novak and Hoffman (1998) conclude from their analysis of Nielsen data that income "has little direct effect on Web use, except for those with either home or work access at the higher income brackets" (p. 13). Instead, Web use is shown to be linked more directly to level of education. This conclusion is supported by Birdsell's study ("Defining the

Technology Gap," 1998), which further established a relationship between educational attainment and use of the World Wide Web: "Of people with an undergraduate degree or higher, 53 percent use the Web while only 19 percent of people with a high school education or less are Web users" ("Defining the Technology Gap," 1998, p. 2).

A broader snapshot of the digital divide with respect to educational background can be found in the three Commerce Department reports. Data from the three reports consistently correlate telephone, PC, and modem penetration rates with levels of education. The higher one's level of education, the more likely one is to have a phone, a computer, and a modem in service. In its latest report, the Department of Commerce reports that individuals with college degrees are more likely to have a telephone than those without a high school education (97.8 percent versus 93.2 percent). Remarkably, those with a college education are nine times more likely than those without any high school to own a PC (68.7 percent versus 7.9 percent). The gap in on-line access is especially pronounced among those with a college degree (48.9 percent), those with a high school diploma (16.3 percent), and those with no high school education whatsoever (3.1 percent) (1999).

Geography
The first decade of the twentieth century saw nearly 10 percent of American households enjoy basic telephone service (*Universal Service*, 1997, p. 1). A nascent concept of universal service—"everyone, everywhere"—evolved over the next quarter century, climaxing in the first comprehensive piece of congressional legislation dealing with the telecommunications industry, the Communications Act of 1934. The rapid expansion of basic telephone service to remote areas of the country was as much a part of AT&T's corporate strategy to improve market share, however, as it was of enlightened social policy. Penetration of telephone service, which had reached almost 40 percent in 1934, exceeded 93 percent nationwide at the end of the twentieth century.

Today, despite the ubiquity of telephone infrastructure and wiring, where one lives—particularly for poor and minority households—can profoundly affect one's access to NII. The extreme poor—under $5,000—in inner cities (79.8 percent) and rural areas (81.6 percent) were significantly below the national average in telephone penetration in 1994. By 1998, both areas experienced declines in penetration rates (78.8 percent and 76.7 percent, respectively). The rural poor had the lowest rate of PC ownership (4.5 percent) in 1994, but that percentage, still lowest when compared with inner-city and urban areas, increased to 11.9 percent by 1998. Poor rural households also hold the distinction for the lowest modem penetration rates (1.1, 2.3, and 4.3 percent) in 1994, 1997, and 1998, respectively (Department of Commerce, 1995, 1998, 1999).

Rural and inner-city minorities are also relatively "unconnected." In 1994 and again in 1997, the lowest telephone penetration rates belonged to rural other non-Hispanic households (Native Americans, Asian Americans, and Eskimos) at 75.5 percent and 76.4 percent, respectively. Rural black and Hispanic households had similarly low telephone rates for both years. Rural and inner-city blacks had the lowest rates of computer ownership (6.4 percent and 10.4 percent in 1994; 17.9 percent and 21.8 percent in 1998). In 1998, rural and inner-city black households fell behind other non-Hispanic households with the lowest modem penetration rates at 7.1 percent and 10.2 percent, respectively.

That the information have-nots are disproportionately found in inner-city areas further complicates an already serious problem with urban core economies. Telephone and cable companies have made substantial telecommunications investment in the outer suburbs, edge cities, and high-tech parks, where there are often tax incentives and greater amenities, while poor, inner-city neighborhoods are not upgraded, thus facing population losses and a reduction in basic services and amenities. An Office of Technology Assessment report (1995) forecast a stark scenario: "The economies of many older, higher-cost metropolitan areas, as well as central cities and older inner suburbs of many [metropolitan areas], are likely to face increasing job loss and disinvestment, leading to underutilization of the built environment, potentially reduced central city agglomeration benefits for industry, increased poverty and ghettoization for residents, particularly minorities, and fiscal problems for local governments" (cited in Clement and Shade, 1996, p. 4).

Household Type

Family structure, too, is a significant variable in predicting access to NII, according to the most recent findings of the Department of Commerce (1999). Married couples with children are above the national average in telephone penetration (96 percent) and are twice as likely to own personal computers and modems (61.8 percent and 39.3 percent, respectively) as are single-parent households of either sex.

Single male households trail the national average in telephone penetration at 86.9 percent. PC and modem penetration rates stand at 30.5 percent and 14 percent, respectively. Similarly, single female households have a telephone penetration rate of 85 percent and PC and modem rates of 31.7 percent and 15 percent, respectively.

Physical Disabilities

A growing number of students with disabilities are entering institutions of higher education for the first time. Hilton-Chalfee and Castorina (1991) theorize that growth is due "in part to advances in medical technology that make it possible for more students with severe disabilities to attend school. It is also due to a greater commitment by K–12 school systems to integrate students with disabilities into mainstream classes and to provide them with necessary support services to insure educational equity" (p. 2). Precise data on individuals with exclusively physical disabilities are difficult to ascertain, as most data-collecting agencies do not—or cannot—distinguish between physical disabilities and various learning disorders that may or may not have a neurological basis. According to the U. S. Census Bureau, the overall disability rate in the United States is 19.4 percent of the population. The bureau identifies 30 groups with specific disabilities, including blindness, cerebral palsy, deafness, learning disability, mental or emotional problem, speech disorder, and "other" (*Americans with Disabilities*, 1991–92). Similar data are available from the National Center for Health Statistics (Centers for Disease Control) [http://www.cdc.gov/nchswww/faq/disable1.html] and the International Center for Health Statistics [http://web.icdi.wvu.edu/disability/ustabl5.html].

The only source of longitudinal data on college students with disabilities is the Cooperative Institutional Research

Program, which began collecting such information from full-time, first-time college freshmen in 1978. The results are published every three years (since 1988) by HEATH Resource Center in *College Freshmen with Disabilities: A Statistical Profile,* which reports that 9.2 percent (or 140,000+) of all college freshmen report having some type of disability, up significantly from 2.6 percent in 1978 (Henderson, 1995). Students with hidden disabilities (learning, health, and other) account for more than half of all freshmen with disabilities. Moreover, men are more likely than women to have learning or speech disabilities, but women outnumber men in every other disability category. Based on current trends, Lissner predicts that "the number of students with disabilities on campus can be expected to continue to grow until this population represents 10% to 15% of the students on any given campus" (1997, p. 1).

For physically disabled students, success in college requires access not only to traditional learning environments such as classrooms, laboratories, and libraries but also increasingly to the tools and other artifacts of information technology. Two laws in particular have established accessibility guidelines for colleges and universities. The Rehabilitation Act of 1973 mandated that educational programs (preschool to postsecondary) receiving federal funding must be physically accessible to students with physical disabilities. The subsequent Americans with Disabilities Act (ADA) of 1990 extended the coverage of the Rehabilitation Act to the private sector as well as to recipients of federal funding.

Federal legislation and various regulations do not specifically address the issue of technological access in higher education. Nonetheless, a practical set of guidelines has emerged from recent case law. Courts have consistently ruled that disabled individuals are entitled to participate in the most integrated academic setting possible, whether it be classroom, laboratory, library, or dormitory *(United States* v. *The University of Alabama,* 908 F.2d. 740 [1990]; *Southeastern Community College* v. *Davis,* 442 U. S. 406 [1979]). Lissner (1997) has identified some of the specific adaptations courts have upheld: "sign language interpreters, adaptive technology in the classroom, adapted laboratory equipment, test format modifications, adaptive telecommunications devices, and the provision of information in alternative formats (Braille, tape, and so on)" (p. 3).

Access to NII for students with physical disabilities requires at least two distinct strategies. First are adaptive technologies built into hardware and operating systems, making them accessible to those individuals with or without specialized needs. Clement and Shade (1996) quotes Goldberg's useful analogy to understand the concept of universal design, which underlies adaptive technologies: "It wasn't long after sidewalks began to be redesigned for wheelchair users that the benefits of curbcuts began to be realized by other people. Parents with strollers, skateboarders, bicycle riders, and delivery people helped prove the point that 'a sidewalk with a curbcut is simply a better sidewalk'" (p. 5). "Electronic curbcuts," best initiated early in a college's development of Web resources, have the collateral benefit of helping a college fulfill its legal responsibility under Title II of the ADA (Vasquez, 1999, p. 4).

A second strategy is the use of assistive technology, which is "any item, piece of equipment, or product system whether acquired off the shelf, modified, or customized that is used to increase, maintain or improve functional capabilities of individuals with disabilities" (Vasquez, 1999, p. 5). Conventional types of technology, of course, are keyboards, mice, modems, microphones, and scanners. Assistive types of technology, however, are on-screen keyboards, braille displays, text-to-voice output, speech recognition, screen readers, screen enlargement software, and scan and read software. A screen reader, for instance, permits a blind student to "read" Web pages using software that verbalizes the text contained on each Web page. As Tim Berners-Lee, W3C director and inventor of the World Wide Web, expressed it, "The power of the Web is in its universality. Access by everyone regardless of disability is an essential aspect" (Vasquez, 1999, p. 4).

Learning Disabilities

Among full-time, first-term students reporting disabilities, the largest growth, both in number and proportion, is among students with learning disabilities. By 1994, these students accounted for 3 percent of all college freshmen; of all students with disabilities, approximately one-third listed a learning disability. In 1991, these figures were 2 and 25 percent, respectively. Between 1988 and 1994, the percentage of freshmen with disabilities who reported a learning disability more than doubled, increasing from 15.3 percent to 32.2 percent (Henderson, 1995).

In 1975, Public Law 94–142, the Education for All Handicapped Children Act, included a definition of learning disability for children necessary to establish guidelines within a K–12 environment. Learning disabilities persist into adulthood, however, and many educators, federal agencies, advocacy groups, and professional organizations have attempted to place the concept of a learning disability within the context of a lifelong condition. One useful definition, formulated by the Interagency Committee on Learning Disabilities, allows for the presence of learning disabilities at any age.

> Learning disabilities *is a generic term that refers to a heterogeneous group of disorders manifested by significant difficulties in acquisition and use of listening, speaking, reading, writing, reasoning, or mathematical abilities, or of social skills. These disorders are intrinsic to the individual and presumed to be due to central nervous system dysfunction. Even though a learning disability may occur concomitantly with other handicapping conditions (e.g. sensory impairment, mental retardation, social and emotional disturbance), with socio-environmental influences (e.g. cultural differences, insufficient or inappropriate instructional psychogenic factors), and especially attention deficit disorder, all of which may cause learning problems, a learning disability is not the direct result of these conditions or influences.* (National Adult Literacy, 1998, p. 2)

The advantage of such a definition is that it provides a foundation of understanding for faculty and administrators who must assist their institutions to satisfy compliance requirements under Section 504 of the Rehabilitation Act of 1973 and under the ADA. A disadvantage of the definition is its broadness and its potential for misapplication. Some college officials have expressed concerns that approving differential treatment for students with questionably diagnosed "invisible" or "hidden" disabilities will compromise academic integrity. As one Boston University official lamented in a letter to the editor of *The Chronicle of Higher Education,*

"Higher education is seriously threatened by a strong advocacy movement that often pays little attention to the validity of learning-disability diagnoses" ("When Students Have Learning Disabilities," 1998, p. A8). Most faculty attitudes, however, fall between the extremes of active resistance and passive acceptance (Leyser, 1989). A large majority, in fact, "are willing to accommodate students with learning disabilities but struggle with ethical concerns in balancing the rights of students with learning disabilities with the academic integrity of the course, program, and institution" (Scott, 1997, p. 86).

Under federal law, faculty are expected to make equitable accommodation through a negotiated process of what is "reasonable" that takes place among faculty, student, and appropriate compliance officer (Scott, 1997). Federal law does not, for instance, require that faculty lower the standards or alter the nature of the course or the program being provided. It does, however, require faculty to thoughtfully reconsider essential course requirements, outcomes, and methods of assessment and to make individual accommodations to the degree possible without compromising academic integrity.

Fair and equal access to computing and information technology fall under the purview of the same federal laws, even though regulations do not specifically address the issue of technological access. Meaningful access includes notice, facilities access, adaptive devices, documentation, and technical support (Lissner, 1997). Institutions are required to give notice of procedures so that disabled students can request accommodations, requests can be evaluated, and appropriate arrangements can be made. Access to facilities goes beyond mere access to a building; it also includes access to the same technologies in the most integrated setting possible. Furthermore, reasonable requests for adaptive devices must be honored. Documentation refers to manuals, procedures, and other training materials in alternate formats accessible to the learning disabled. Technical support for current technologies must also be available to the learning disabled.

Summary
In the very near future, Americans will require access to NII for purposes of employment, entertainment, and citizenship. Trends such as electronic mail and commerce,

telecommuting and telemedicine, media-enhanced and distance education, digital libraries and digital government confirm the essential direction toward which our information society is moving. Continued disengagement from the new information technologies based on one's age, income, race, gender, education, location, household, or physical or cognitive disabilities will have profound societal consequences from which no one will be exempt. Higher education, to no less a degree than other major American institutions, must remove barriers to access—in this case, for nontraditional students and lifelong learners—without sacrificing quality. The solutions will be costly and complicated, but the alternatives will be catastrophic.

Problems of access have been exacerbated in recent years by economic trends outside the control, if not the influence, of colleges and universities. Two trends in particular threaten to deprive millions of students of the social and economic benefits of a postsecondary education. The first trend is the steady erosion of state and federal discretionary aid. On the federal level, mandatory spending on such entitlement programs as Social Security and Medicaid has consumed a growing proportion of the federal budget since 1965. According to the Congressional Budget Office, entitlement programs will account for nearly three-quarters of federal budget expenditures by 2005 *(Breaking the Social Contract,* 1997). On the state level, lawmakers are allocating proportionally larger shares of annual expenditures to health and human services and, increasingly, to law enforcement and public safety, leaving higher education to draw from residual funds that must be shared with the K–12 system, transportation, statewide revenue sharing, and general government operating expenses. And colleges and universities can expect this pattern of reduced public support to continue until academics abandon their reluctance to influence lawmakers and make their case for increased funding (Lederman, 1998).

A second trend is actually a corollary to the national trend in income, reported in the last section as predictive of technological access. The growing disparity between the top and bottom percentiles of wage and family income in the United States, it was noted, has contributed to a society of technological haves and have-nots (Department of Commerce, 1995, 1998, 1999; Gladieux and Swail, 1999). The corollary of this trend is that more and more families have to assign a greater and greater share of personal income to higher education to compensate for the decline in real wages. Add to this domestic dilemma a tuition growth rate fueled in no small part by necessary technological enhancements in administration and instruction, and the goal of mass—much less universal—access to higher education becomes greatly imperiled.

As many families alter their own priorities to pay for college, senior campus administrators grapple with exploding demand for high-performance computing and rising expectations that complete support services will be available. Market Data Retrieval, an educational information firm,

The growing disparity between the top and bottom percentiles of wage and family income in the United States has contributed to a society of technological haves and have-nots.

conservatively estimates that $2.8 billion was spent on technology at two- and four-year colleges and universities during the 1997–98 school year ("High Tech Adds to High Cost," 1998). Of that estimate, $1.2 billion (43 percent) was spent on academic hardware, $800 million (29 percent) on administrative hardware, $309 million (11 percent) on administrative software, and $356 million (13 percent) on academic software. The latter estimate for academic software is considered conservative because, in part, it does not reflect purchases buried in departmental budgets. Furthermore, these numbers do not reflect funds expended for faculty and staff training, personnel and user support, Web server management, maintenance, depreciation, scheduled replacement, security, and so forth. A number of institutions are planning substantial increases in general fund support for technology infrastructure development and enhancements. In fact, one study suggests that the percentage of institutional operating budgets devoted to information technology has doubled, and in some cases tripled, during the 1990s (Ringle, 1997).

Many observers expect technology to theoretically reduce or at least stabilize the long-term costs of instruction despite enormous initial outlays and expensive continuous upgrades. Assuming "no significant difference" in learning outcomes between technologically mediated and traditional instruction, observers reason that new technologies, like asynchronous Web-based instruction, can "scale up," that is, serve increasingly larger numbers of students with smaller marginal costs. In a series of case studies evaluating the costs and benefits of technologically mediated instruction, however, Jewett (1999) convincingly demonstrates that too many barriers presently exist within and between institutions to achieve the necessary economies of scale. The very large numbers of students required to generate these economies would require levels of faculty collaboration and interinstitutional cooperation not often embraced in a system as diverse and autonomous as American higher education (Karelis, 1999).

Institutions attempting to overcome these "scale barriers" are discovering a host of issues that must be addressed: (1) mission and vision, (2) collaboration and cooperation, (3) price and cost, (4) tangible and intangible costs, and (5) student technology fees and leasing arrangements.

Mission and Vision

As more and more colleges and universities explore the pedagogical implications of the Internet and the World Wide Web, traditional distinctions between distance education and residential instruction are beginning to fade. The ubiquity of digital technologies necessitates a reconsideration of target markets so that institutional mission comes under review at the same time that a new vision of learning emerges.

Reconceptualizing institutional mission

Linking institutional mission to fiscal planning is part of a larger education reform effort to improve efficiency through differentiation. Colleges and universities are being challenged by government agencies and advocacy groups to "pursue greater mission differentiation to streamline their services and better respond to the changing needs of their constituencies" (*Breaking the Social Contract,* 1997, p. 16). Within integrated statewide systems of higher education, mission differentiation is intended to keep mission creep and duplication of programs to a minimum. Creep occurs when community colleges take on the mantle of baccalaureate institutions, when state universities attempt to become centers of research, and when research universities provide remedial instruction.

Technological mission creep—trying to stay apace of skyrocketing user demands by investing in every conceivable technology and hybrid available—can have profoundly negative economic consequences for institutions attempting to address simultaneously other pressing budgetary concerns such as financial aid, personnel compensation, and deferred maintenance. A successful financial model for technology "must be designed with sensitivity to what is possible and practicable, given an institution's financial constraints" (Ringle, 1997, p. 22). In the zero-sum game of education finance, some institutions may be able to afford new technology systems and services only as they sacrifice funding from other areas of the budget.

The role of leadership

The role of technology leadership in "articulating a clear understanding of how technology fits into the overall institutional strategy and what this implies for the total funding picture" (Ringle, 1997, p. 24) cannot be overestimated. But understanding, it is assumed, precedes articulation. Technology leaders must achieve and promote understanding by expanding participation in fiscal planning to the full range of technology users.

> *Technology financial planning is all too often a backroom exercise conducted by the chief technology officer, alone or with a small group of trusted colleagues. Such planning does absolutely nothing to moderate user demand nor to promote understanding of the limitations faced by the information technology organization. The more awareness that users have of information financial constraints, the better. It is important that a financial strategy reflect, to as great degree as possible, technology needs as perceived by users. A user endorsement of the financial plan for technology, based on an understanding of fiscal limitations, may help to garner new institutional resources while it helps—at least temporarily—to moderate user demand.* (Ringle, 1997, p. 27)

Innovation theorists describe how leaders facilitate such critical elements of planning as "gathering information, communicating with other members of the organization, developing new coalitions, and identifying existing coalitions that perceive their members as stakeholders in the process" (Curry, 1992, p. 24). In professional organizations such as colleges and universities, communication and decision making must be two-directional, or such innovations made possible by technology will not permeate the organization from top to bottom (James, James, and Ashe, 1990). In short, "the measure of organization members' commitment to change is related directly to the extent of their participation in decisions governing the process" (Curry, 1992, p. 25).

Environmental scanning
Once leadership addresses the issue of participatory fiscal planning, a reconceptualization of institutional mission becomes the common focus. Any technology acquisition and implementation decisions must be made within the context of internally directed or externally mandated mission differentiation. The point is that tools exist that institutions can

use to map the market of postsecondary education, to find their places within it, and to identify what steps need to be taken.

One tool is *environmental scanning,* "a widely accepted technique for monitoring the pulse of change in the external environment, whether it be in political, economic, technological, or social arenas or of national or international importance" (*Environmental Scanning,* 1996, p. 1). From a strategic and fiscal point of view, environmental scanning "lessens the randomness of information used in decision-making and alerts managers to trends and issues that may affect the organization" (p. 1). A correct scan of the external environment can assist educators in determining students' learning needs and in marketing programs created to meet those needs.

An exemplary environmental scanning program may be found at the University of Georgia Center for Continuing Education. Since 1985, more than 60 faculty, administrators, and staff have routinely scanned documents and various resources looking for trends and issues of strategic importance for continuing higher education. The Georgia Center now distributes *Lookout,* an environmental scanning newsletter, twice yearly; the newsletter is available to download at http://gactr.uga.edu/scanning.

Market taxonomy
Another useful tool is a *market taxonomy,* such as the one developed by the Institute for Research on Higher Education at the University of Pennsylvania (Zemsky, Shaman, and Iannozzi, 1997). A series of calculations based on four sets of information—admit and yield rates, percentage of freshmen who graduate with a B.A. or B.S. in five years, percentage of undergraduate enrollment that is part time, and the ratio of the numbers of B.A. and B.S. degrees awarded to total undergraduate enrollment—permit institutions to determine their positions along a horizontal continuum. The market segments making up the continuum range from "convenience/user-friendly" institutions ("colleges and universities that teach large numbers of part-time and intermittent students who may or may not be seeking a degree" [p. 25]) to "name brand" institutions ("a limited set of highly selective, very competitive institutions that provide their graduates with a kind of *medallion,* whose principal labor

market value is realized upon matriculation to a graduate or professional school" [p. 26]). In between the two extremes are segments representing rather selective public and private institutions that, more often than not, serve local or metropolitan markets. Members of these market segments suffer the distinction, to a greater or lesser degree, of trying to serve learners at both extremes of the continuum: traditional, full-time students and nontraditional, part-time older adults.

Because the data needed to determine one's market segment are available by completing the calculations indicated earlier, what remains for an institution is to identify its market niche and to ask and then answer questions of a strategic nature: "What should we do to move up in our current segment or to shift to a segment more congenial with our aspirations?" (p. 33). Postsecondary institutions are notoriously poor at using the kinds of information available through research-based marketing. Such marketing consultation has generally been available for decades to a variety of customers, and it now behooves institutions that are having difficulty conducting market research or choosing between competing strategies to seek such expertise from within the ranks of informed faculty or from outside the institution.

A vision of learning

Successful fiscal planning depends not only on reconceptualizing the mission and target market(s) of the institution but also on developing a focused, coherent, and common vision of what the institution "thinks the learning process could be like given the broad adoption of technology" (North Central Regional Technology in Education Consortium, 1997, p. 1). Without such a vision, there is little hope that the new media will contribute measurably to improved student learning and could conceivably, given the enormous costs allocated, wreck the institution financially on the shoals of implementation.

In the process of creating and sharing such a vision, technology discussants must distinguish, as it were, the media from the message. A shared vision of learning begins not with hardware and software needed but with consideration of the skills and competencies students need to learn, what teaching-learning strategies are best—"especially those that would not even be feasible without the newer technologies" (Ehrmann, 1995, p. 24), and what specific technologies are best for supporting those teaching-learning strategies. Such a focus lays the foundation for fiscal planning for technology.

Collaboration and Cooperation

Possibly the most powerful lever in moving vision to reality, within a framework of realistic cost containment, is collaborative effort. American culture has always embraced individuality and autonomy as part of its "pioneering spirit," but in recent years the costs associated with developing and implementing new technology require a new metaphor, one emphasizing interdependence and complementarity (Austin and Baldwin, 1991). The direct benefits of intra- and interinstitutional technology collaboration include program articulation, delivery system integration, reduced duplication, maximization of limited resources, and preservation of underenrolled course offerings (Gatliff and Wendel, 1998). In American higher education, collaboration takes three distinct forms: intrainstitutional, interinstitutional, and academic and private sector cooperation.

Intrainstitutional collaboration: "unbundling" faculty roles and responsibilities

The most controversial cost-containment strategy yet proposed is to reduce labor intensity by employing new and emerging technologies to absorb more and more of the teaching function (Young, 1997b). Restructuralists point to the fact that approximately 80 percent of an institution's expenditures are attributable to personnel costs (Twigg, 1994c), a ripe target for reform-minded budget analysts. Historically, the teaching function has evolved into at least five separate roles: course designer, lecturer, discussion moderator, counselor, and evaluator (Boettcher, 1998a; Young, 1997b). Joint ventures among faculty content specialists, librarians, publishers, instructional designers, and software specialists are bringing to market a range of products that will inevitably and dramatically affect the teaching function.

One salutary illustration of intrainstitutional cooperation is worth noting here. Pennsylvania State University's Project Vision library studies course, Learning Strategies for the Information Age, is a model of faculty and staff cooperation at one institution (Harvey and Dewald, 1997). In this course, faculty work alongside academic librarians and technical support personnel "to expand the traditional content of library literacy sessions by incorporating critical thinking, evaluating resources, and computer searching skills" (p. 1). By partnering with librarians, teaching faculty can dramatically enrich course content, learning outcomes, teaching strategies, and media production. In reality, however, the literature on instructional technology and development, dating back to at least the 1960s, has always talked about the use of teams to collaborate on these types of projects. The concept is not new, but teams have caught on only sparingly.

Nevertheless, "unbundling" the teaching function, in the jargon of the day—that is, breaking up and distributing the various faculty responsibilities—presents a challenge to the academy, especially when it involves for-profit vendors of educational materials. If we closely examine its culture, we observe that faculty have shown flexibility in the past by adapting to such technologies as printed textbooks written, for example, by well-respected economists and then distributed by for-profit publishers. "But these same teachers would . . . be much less willing to have videotapes of these world-famous economists replace them at the lectern, even if it meant that they could concentrate on supervising undergraduate research and other high-status tasks. The 'not invented here' syndrome seems to afflict certain aspects of teaching, but not others" (Karelis, 1999, p. 24). Critics are quick to point out, however, that such a step would only further centralize control of course content and evaluation, undermine intellectual autonomy and independence, and threaten careers. Pressures to cut labor costs have already increased the proportion of part-time to full-time faculty (*Straight Talk*, 1998), and increased virtualization of the teaching function is likely to exacerbate this trend.

Interinstitutional collaboration
A two-year study by the Commission on National Investment in Higher Education (*Breaking the Social Contract*, 1997) concludes that if colleges and universities are serious about improving productivity, a sharing of resources through mission differentiation is necessary and inevitable. Specifically, the commission recommends:

1. Seamless alignment of undergraduate requirements;
2. Pooling of introductory courses and instructors;

3. Joint outsourcing of service functions, ranging from health care to physical plant maintenance to vendor contracts;
4. Shared infrastructure; and
5. Shared library holdings and resources.

All of these recommendations, commissioners note, can be accomplished through cooperative use of administrative and instructional technology.

In many states, legislatures have stressed the need for institutions to more fully exploit available technology resources instead of constantly having to reinvent the wheel. One state legislator best expressed an overarching incentive for institutions to share resources: "They know that if they work together they will have a better chance of accessing whatever funding there is around here at the state level" (Ruppert, 1997, p. 20). "Ironically," notes Ruppert, who interviewed 21 state "education and technology" legislators from 11 states, "it may be that to some extent state legislatures' largely decentralized funding approach, which has given campuses considerable autonomy in purchasing decisions and network development, has contributed to exacerbating interinstitutional competition and interconnectivity problems" (pp. 21–22). Now, it appears, many legislatures are attempting to bring under control hemorrhaging institutional expenditures brought about largely through replication of educational services.

One plan to begin interinstitutional cooperation is through technologically mediated team teaching. The advantages of such teaming are many, particularly for institutions heavily involved in distributed education:

By combining efforts, faculty from different institutions can expand course offerings and provide those courses to a greater number of students, thus becoming less dependent upon the limitations of on-campus registration. Team members benefit from the experience of working with peers, as instruction is improved through capitalizing on the respective strengths of each member and by developing new knowledge and skills. Students also enjoy benefits, such as expanded course offerings, stimulation from technologies used in distance education, the expertise of team teachers, and the opportunity to receive instruction that may only be available through distance education. (Gatliff and Wendel, 1998, pp. 61–62)

A number of formidable obstacles stand in the way of widespread adoption of technologically mediated team teaching. Problems of miscommunication, unfair distribution of labor, unilateral decision making, uncoordinated administrative and technical support, and other considerations make thorough planning an absolutely critical prerequisite to such interinstitutional collaboration.

Some states and regions of the country are pursuing collaborative arrangements more aggressively than others. For example, the Virginia Community College System of 23 colleges has developed, beginning in 1992, formal policies, procedures, standards, and management practices for sharing instructors and courses among the colleges.

In California, colleges and universities are expected to absorb another half a million new college students by 2006 (Finney, 1997). The staggering construction and operating costs that will be required to provide essentially the same level of service have caused the California Higher Education Policy Center and other agencies to recommend admissions reform as well as greater opportunities for early campus enrollment. Finney cites a 1973 Carnegie Commission report, *Continuity or Discontinuity,* in which leading educators at that time "called attention to the overlap and duplication that occurred during the last two years of high school and the first two years of college, suggesting that the last year of high school be eliminated for most students. Few changes in the contemporary reform movement would invalidate the critique of the Carnegie Commission more than twenty-five years ago" (p. 2).

State and regional technology initiatives now evolve quickly and take many distinct forms. Although the initial vision of Western Governors' University has been slow to materialize for various reasons, the number of participating institutions in the Southern Regional Electronic Campus (SREC) more than tripled, from 40 to 150, during 1998. Strong student demand, it would appear, has prompted an increase in available classes, from 900 in 1998 to more than 1,250 by spring 1999. The number of degree programs— associate, bachelor's, and master's—is expected to grow during the same period from 25 to 60 ("On Line," 1998, A16). The growth of such consortia challenges traditional assumptions about boundaries and service districts and "about tuition policy and interstate competition among tax-supported institutions" (Blumenstyk, 1998a, p. A16). But there is more to the story. First, participation (at least in some states) was very strictly controlled initially. The recent growth was as much a factor of the removal of these controls as a response to growth in the number of students. Second, enrollments directly attributable to the SREC are difficult to measure, and the reported numbers are somewhat suspect. Distance education enrollments at the participating institutions have grown, but it probably has little to do with the SREC at this point. In fact, the growth being reported is also attributable to the increased number of participating institutions. This is a very knee-jerk, me-too arrangement rather than a true response by states or institutions to deal with the bigger issues of demand, service area boundaries, and so forth. The SREC is now trying to work out these issues, but it is not yet close to a solution. A more interesting implication, however, is that the genie is out of the bottle. The SREC cannot take too many steps backward without having to face at least some of these issues. It simply cannot pretend the problems do not exist. Some spinoffs have even been created in an attempt to control turf. Virginia, for example, created the Virginia Electronic Campus, modeled after the SREC with many of the same institutions and courses. Even though administrators talk about eliminating turf battles and boundaries, the "map" has just been changed—and the concept of borders is still alive and well.

On another front, the Community College Distance Learning Network (CCDLN), which includes eight cutting-edge two-year colleges in six states, expects to market as many as 500 courses delivered via the Internet, telecourses, or hybrid technology (Blumenstyk, 1998a, A16). The aggressive posture of both SREC and CCDLN comes partly in response to years of territorial encroachment by such for-profit entities as the University of Phoenix and DeVries.

Academic and private sector cooperation
Higher education in the United States represents a 175 to several hundred billion dollar a year market (Hooker, 1997;

Noble, 1998). Digital technologies, advocates contend, will transform higher education in the coming years, making the academy more accessible, more affordable, and more effective. Skeptics, however, are not so sure and express concern that the kinds of joint ventures between not-for-profit academic institutions and private sector business entities are leading to greater and greater commercialization of the academic function, with uncertain consequences for students (Cordes, 1998; Monaghan, 1998).

First and foremost among categories of private sector participation would be textbook publishers. Publishers have become increasingly important to faculty for software support and for the often elaborate websites created to supplement their textbooks. Many faculty find the course management software, test banks, and analysis components indispensable but available only to instructors who agree to select specific publishers' texts. Publishers' websites also often include tools faculty can use to easily build or display their own course-specific components. The costs for the publishers are passed on to students through textbook prices. The sites are often far more elaborate and rich than most faculty could ever develop on their own.

Another type of venture includes institutional cooperation with software vendors. UCLA Extension, the largest single-campus continuing higher education program in the country, for example, has partnered with OnlineLearning.net to provide continuing education opportunities to approximately 2,000 students since fall 1996 (Lucas, 1998). UCLA provides the faculty and the course content, and OnlineLearning.net offers software programs as well as technical support to customers (students). "Their typical student is a 43-year-old woman, with a $73K household income, who is looking for a career change or career enhancement. Both organizations see students as clients and so have a customer service orientation" (p. 16).

Similarly, Marygrove College, a Catholic liberal arts college founded by a religious order more than 150 years ago, recently partnered with Canter and Associates, "a for-profit producer and disseminator of educational courseware for K–12 teachers and . . . [a provider of] educational [materials] to assist classroom teachers" (Lee and Marsh, 1998, p. 44). The Canter-Marygrove partnership presently serves 3,000 practicing classroom teachers in a comprehensive distance education master's degree program.

Among the compelling concerns for educators about such alliances is one that has received little attention in the literature: can cultural differences between entirely distinct entities with completely different missions share a single goal—to provide a high-quality educational experience for students? After all, as Lee and Marsh frame the analogy, "A collaboration between partners from such diverse 'backgrounds' is like a marriage between individuals from differing cultures; all may eat dinner together, but the rules about the dinner rituals, and even what is eaten, vary greatly" (p. 45).

Price and Cost

When the National Commission on the Cost of Higher Education began to investigate the phenomenon of rising college tuition in 1996, one of the first obstacles it faced was basic terminology. Overcoming the confusion associated with multiple and often interchangeable uses of "cost" and "price" became "a major semantic challenge" for the commission, resulting in a final report that devotes two and one-half pages to painstaking definition (*Straight Talk*, 1998, pp. 5–7).

Determining the price and cost of campus information technology is an equally elusive undertaking. One of the prevailing myths is the idea that "the cost of technology is its purchase price" (Task Force on Technology in Higher Education, 1996, p. 17). Nothing could be further from the truth. Oberlin (1996b) makes this useful distinction: "The price of technology is what you pay to purchase it. The cost includes the price as well as all the other expenses associated with owning, operating, and maintaining it" (p. 26). And the costs can be staggeringly high—as much as ten times the purchase price, according to one estimate (Gartner Groups, Inc., cited in Oberlin, p. 27).

The cost of today's technology must be defined in terms emphasizing its fluidity, rather than its fixity. The word *infrastructure* conveys a sense of permanence, especially as applied to physical plant. *Technological infrastructure,* however, is more evanescent and includes building wiring, fiber runs, electronics, main campus servers—including Web servers, public lab servers, and library (Online Public

Access Catalog and database) servers—desktop computers, peripherals such as printers, scanners, and projection devices, and, of course, furniture. Unlike bricks and mortar and concrete and steel, technological infrastructure must be constantly serviced. According to Leach and Smallen (1998), the costs of servicing information technology fall into two categories: "those that deal with the care and feeding of the infrastructure and those that provide the related support services" (p. 38).

> *Infrastructure-related services involve aspects of acquiring, installing, maintaining, and replacing things on an annual basis. Whether the replacement costs are part of the annual operating budget or are to be viewed as deferred maintenance (as many colleges have done in repair of their building infrastructure), they are real costs related to providing the necessary IT services. As such, they must be considered as part of any analysis of the cost of providing these important services.* (p. 38)

A good illustration of the changing nature of infrastructure is the miles of unused fiber planted deep in the ductwork of administrative offices, classrooms, and residence halls in the late 1980s. Fiber Distributed Data Interface (FDDI) was thought to be the future of campus networking (Ringle and Updegrove, 1998). Although still used at some locales, FDDI has been largely superseded by such alternative technologies as asynchronous transfer mode and fast Ethernet. The current and future demands of multimedia technologies and high-performance computing make network upgrades ongoing.

Support services, on the other hand, are "those areas in which budget components are largely staff driven and relate to provision of support to users of the infrastructure" (Leach and Smallen, 1998, p. 39). A cursory glance at college and university websites from around the nation suggests that staff support centers have been developed for some or all of the following academic and administrative services:

- Instructional development services that support the incorporation of new technologies into the curriculum;

- Network services that operate and maintain instructional computing labs, computer-equipped classrooms and libraries, and Web servers;
- Telecommunications services that operate and maintain campus telephone systems and voice mail;
- Business services that support general payroll, purchasing, human resource management, and campus facilities; and
- Public safety services that secure premises, dispatch campus police and the local fire department, and coordinate ambulance response to campus.

A fundamental misconception about the value of and demand for IT, stemming principally from a philosophical conflict between old and new ways of managing information, is likely to result in significant underestimation of costs. In the "old" days of mainframe culture, from the 1960s through the 1980s, only an isolated minority of technical specialists or data entry clerks had access to the technology. Administrators, faculty, and staff outside the loop—in this case, the management information systems loop—had virtually no access to computer technology, except indirectly through whatever batch printouts specialists made available. This *legacy* system, as it has come to be known, was a stable, hierarchical, control-oriented model. By the early 1980s, a number of forces were at work to open access to computing. The first was distributed computing made possible by minicomputers. The second was the personal computer, which brought distributed computing right to the desktop (Tapscott and Caston, 1993). The low cost of PCs, coupled with powerful new software applications for individuals and for departments, created for the first time a computing "presence" in virtually every administrative office and academic department. Once networked, PCs permitted unprecedented levels of information exchange, portending significant implications for administrative services, research, and instruction.

"Legacy-based assumptions," however, continue to influence decision making at many institutions (Oberlin, 1996a, p. 12). In lieu of new cost models, institutions continue to rely on "budget and planning processes that, in many cases, are better suited to buying library books or renovating laboratories than to dealing with the short product cycle and unfamiliar jargon of computers and networking" (McCollum, 1997, p. A27). Attempting to remedy the relative dearth of fiscal models within the context of academic institutions, the COSTS project [http://www.its.colgate.edu/kleach/costs] reports on a survey of IT expenditures drawn from more than 100 colleges and universities nationwide, permitting for the first time a clear glimpse of how and in what ways institutions are budgeting for technology. Institutions now have a mechanism with which to compare spending patterns to newly established norms.

One of the striking realities of fiscal planning for distributed computing environments is that costs continue to rise, even as per unit prices of technology decline (Jacobs, 1995; Oberlin, 1996a, 1996b). First, unlike furniture, whose functionality remains fixed, digital technologies evolve in relatively short life cycles. A PC purchased today at yesterday's price of $2,500 has considerably more functionality—greater memory, more powerful processes, more sophisticated software, and more peripherals. Second, the typical computer user, empowered by productivity gains made possible by new technology, will naturally covet a system more powerful than what is available at the replacement cost. For example, peripherals once considered luxuries may now be perceived as necessities. Third, and most important, the useful (read *economic*) life of a computer is over long before it stops working.

An economic life cycle is defined as the useful financial life of an item. In other words, the life cycle is the number of years one should plan to keep a piece of hardware or software. For example, a life cycle of three years for a computer implies that at the end of three years, the computer is either: (1) no longer suited for its intended purpose (e.g., Intel 80286-based servers won't run Netware 3.11), or (2) maintenance and support have grown to the extent that it is cheaper to replace the computer than keep it, or (3) new requirements or performance standards (such as portability, ease of use, user interfaces, visualization, networking, processing power) have necessitated its replacement to meet user needs. Keeping information technology longer than its economic life cycle is a mistake. Not only does it waste current money, but it forfeits the advantages inherent in new technology. (Oberlin, 1996b, p. 28)

The serious difficulty institutions face is staying current and hence competitive. Life cycles are getting shorter; thus, an institutional commitment to replace or refurbish computers every three years may prove inadequate for cutting-edge research and for attracting students with elevated expectations. Financial planning becomes ever more critical.

Tangible Versus Intangible Costs
New costs arising from fuller participation by faculty and students cannot be completely or accurately gauged using today's economic measures. For instance, how do we begin to measure the cost to the institution and to the individual educator who devotes increasing units of time (however calculated) to instructional technology activities and less time to scholarly endeavors? How are tenure and promotion decisions affected? Do personal costs associated with technology participation by innovators and early adopters scale up to the majority of faculty and students? How are faculty fully and fairly compensated for course development using new and emerging technologies? Assigning costs to these and other activities requires new sets of economic tools.

The many new and hybrid forms of distance education elevate issues of time and cost to a new level. Depending on the need of the student and the resources of the institution, at least eight new learning environments, pioneered by distance learning practitioners, are available today on U.S. college and university campuses: (1) one-way audiovisual classrooms, (2) two-way audiovisual classrooms, popularly known as interactive television (ITV), (3) two-way audio classrooms, (4) two-way audio graphic classrooms, (5) desktop groupware conferencing, (6) desktop videoconferencing, (7) asynchronous desktop conferencing, and (8) asynchronous CD-ROM hybrids (Tucker, 1995). Each of these relatively new learning environments has its own start-up and ongoing costs based on infrastructure and support service requirements.

Examining just one of these venues exposes a number of the intangible costs inherent in new forms of technologically mediated instruction. Asynchronous desktop conferencing,

How do we begin to measure the cost to the institution and to the individual educator who devotes increasing units of time to instructional technology activities and less time to scholarly endeavors?

sometimes called Web-based instruction, for example, entails a number of intangible costs that give the lie to the suggestion that quality education can be offered cheaply. Assuming, for example, that all facets of instruction are "bundled," that is, completely under the jurisdiction of a single instructor, course development costs are a function of the time it takes to produce materials adapted to a Web environment. Assuming further a three-hour-per-week, fifteen-week course, each hour of instruction will likely require, by current estimates, an average of eighteen hours of faculty time to create just one hour of instruction on the Web (Boettcher, 1998a). In an "unbundled" approach, where faculty function primarily as content specialists, then technology specialists are responsible for translating content into such interactive formats as computer simulations and digitized problem solving. "We can be fairly confident that if the goal is to build materials that can be delivered multiple times and independent of the designing/developing faculty member, then costs will be dramatically higher than for building materials to be delivered in a 'bundled' environment" (Boettcher, 1998a, p. 58).

Faculty and administrators are already carefully examining shortcuts to the normal development time and costs associated with preparing materials for these new distributed environments. Boettcher (1998a) suggests course templates, kits from textbook publishers, and collaborations and partnerships with other institutions to bring courses to the Web more efficiently and effectively. The critical issue of quality remains the most important factor in determining whether or not to pursue alternative strategies. A ratio of cost to benefit must be carefully established.

Student Technology Fees and Computer Leasing Arrangements

To help cover rising IT costs, more colleges and universities are imposing mandatory IT fees and requiring—or at least strongly recommending—students come to campus with computers or be prepared to lease them at group rates. Although obvious economic benefits accrue to institutions adopting such policies, a number of serious issues arise that require closer examination.

The *1998 National Survey of Information Technology in Higher Education* (Green, 1998) reveals that nearly half

(45.8 percent) of the 571 two- and four-year colleges and universities participating in the survey report a mandatory student IT fee, up from 38.5 percent in 1997 and 28.3 percent in 1995. Despite the increasing number of institutions levying such fees, the average fee at public four-year institutions has remained unchanged at $120 for two consecutive years. At community colleges and private four-year colleges, however, fees have risen by one-third, from $55 to $72 and from $112 to $146, respectively.

The problem with IT fees is at least twofold. On the one hand, critics question why costs are not included in tuition, suggesting that such fees "are just thinly disguised tuition hikes. They argue that computing resources are as necessary as libraries and—like library costs—should be rolled into tuition" (Young, 1997a, A23). On the other hand, fiscal planners may succumb to the erroneous notion that student fees for IT should be sufficient to replace institutional investment in IT. As Kenneth Green, director of the Campus Computing Project, makes clear, "Computer networks, user support services, software and content licenses, computer labs and instructional classrooms are key components of the campus technology infrastructure and need more than just student fees to be viable and reliable" (1998, p. 2).

Furthermore, a growing number of postsecondary institutions are requiring—or at least strongly encouraging—students to lease or purchase computers. Currently, only 2 percent of colleges in one study indicated that they require students to own computers ("High Tech Adds to High Cost," 1998). Another study suggests that although computer requirements are fairly common among small private colleges, most state-supported institutions are still "recommending rather than requiring that students come to campus with a computer in tow" (Gates, 1998, p. 1). Several two- and four-year institutions are experimenting with laptop leasing initiatives (Cartwright, 1997; Holleque and Cartwright, 1997).

Variations on the theme of students' owning or leasing computers permeate the landscape of higher education. For example, the University of North Carolina at Chapel Hill required all 3,300 freshmen in fall 2000 to have laptop computers that meet certain specifications. To save money through purchasing in volume and requiring one company for support services, UNC–Chapel Hill made IBM the preferred supplier (Blumenstyk, 1998b). Other institutions, such as Georgia Tech, the University of Florida, and Virginia Tech, are phasing in the requirement for all students to have their own computers (Gates, 1998).

A number of two- and four-year institutions are experimenting with leasing arrangements. For instance, Valley City State University and Mayville State University, two of eleven public colleges and universities in the North Dakota University System, received the approval of the State Board of Higher Education in November 1995 to launch a universal laptop initiative starting with the fall 1996 semester. Because neither university received special state funding for this initiative, both institutions had to depend on a $1.3 million, five-year federal Title III grant as well as a $950 annual student assessment to cover most of the costs of leasing the laptops and software and providing support services. In the first annual survey of results, a substantial majority of students indicated that the initiative had increased their research abilities and marketability to potential employers (Holleque and Cartwright, 1997). A similar laptop leasing initiative is under way at Clayton College and State University and at Floyd College in Georgia (Cundift and Briscar, 1998).

Several problems are associated with arrangements for owning or leasing computers:

1. Will universal access to technology, in and of itself, drive curricular reform without substantial faculty incentives to exploit technology's potential?
2. Will computer literacy requirements be necessary for students?
3. What will be the impact of universal access on computer network infrastructure?
4. What obligation for student support will universal access create?
5. How is the institution to deal with the consequences of the network's crashing at the end of the semester as student papers are due, exam notes need to be accessed, research has to be done, and so forth?
6. What supplemental staff should be hired for the inevitable student calls for assistance as computer use becomes distributed to every room and even to technological neophytes?

7. Would lease or purchase arrangements be more advantageous to students? to the institution? (Some site license agreements require computers to be owned by the institution rather than by students.)
8. What security and maintenance issues must be addressed at the outset?

Summary

Expectations that technology will ultimately reduce or stabilize the long-term costs of instruction are simply unrealistic. A more prudent course begins with a clear understanding of how technology fits into the overall institutional mission and the formulation of a strategic plan. The main strategy should be cost avoidance through mission differentiation by enhancing collaboration and cooperation within the institution and between the institution and the public, by distinguishing the price from the complex costs associated with infrastructure and support services, by overcoming the legacy-based assumptions of the mainframe culture, by determining the economic life cycles of computers and strategically planning their obsolescence, by developing economic tools to gauge the many intangible costs of mass adoption of technology, and by developing a rational and equitable policy on technology fees and computer leasing agreements for incoming students.

ISSUES OF QUALITY AND EFFECTIVENESS

It turns out that learning is not merely a cognitive phenomenon. It is a social phenomenon as well. People need much more than information: they need to know why they are getting this information, how it can be used, how other people use it, how other people understand it. They need support, encouragement, and relevance.
—Stephen Downes (quoted in Repman and Logan, 1996, p. 35)

The enormous educational potential of high-performance and networked computing is threatened, as we have seen, by barriers preventing access to the rich information resources made possible by IT and by increasing costs of servicing and upgrading the campus technology infrastructure. No education technology issue is of greater importance, or more frequently debated, however, than that of quality assurance. In truth, if issues of quality were not so complex and contentious, issues of access and cost would be much less difficult to resolve satisfactorily. Technology advocates and critics alike would nevertheless agree on one point: technologically mediated instruction must not imperil the well-deserved reputation for quality that American higher education has enjoyed both here and abroad.

The accreditation community is in the very early stages of addressing the many challenges to the traditional accreditation process that technology-enhanced and -distributed education has created. In truth, many of these quality issues are the same ones raised for earlier courses using slides and tapes, programmed instruction, mastery learning, and telecourses. As the new computer-based technologies go mainstream, however, a greater sense of urgency to resolve issues old and new press on accreditors. Among the emerging issues of quality assurance identified at a recent conference of the Council for Higher Education Accreditation are a lack of consensus about basic terminology, such as distance education, distributed learning, and technology-enhanced learning; a lack of consistent strategy in organizing a response to the many new and hybrid forms of distributed education; the changing definition of faculty roles and responsibilities; calls for uniform standards while maintaining diversity among institutions; the notion of "cyber-visitations"; and the reconceptualization of semester, class hour, and seat time (*Quality Assurance*, 1998). These and other issues have been placed high on the agendas of accreditors and other professionals working in the higher education policy arena.

The primary beneficiaries of high technology, our students, have not always been well served by institutions trying to saddle the cutting edge but failing to address adequately many of the key quality concerns raised not just by accreditors but also by instructional designers and the early adopters of the technologies themselves. With neither adequate preparation nor sufficient institutional support, many faculty have entered the new learning environments, among them interactive television and Internet-based classes, and essentially replicated traditional teaching methods rather than adapt the methods to take advantage of the new technologies. Theorists and practitioners are coming to recognize that exemplary teaching and learning in today's networked digital culture involve a whole range of pedagogical issues not encountered in the traditional classroom—such as content, design, assessment, and support.

The Content Dilemma

The growth and availability of Internet-based resources furnish students with a stunning array of options with which to locate information and publish it electronically. The World Wide Web, the Internet's interactive multimedia delivery system, provides access to text, images, video, and sound files from Web servers across town or around the world. An increasing number of savvy, computer-literate college students come to campus already familiar with the nuances of electronic mail, discussion groups (for example, Usenet Newsgroups), real-time chat (for example, Internet Relay Chat), multiuser interactive virtual reality sites such as MUDs and MOOs, and hypertext, hypermedia websites. For many students, the Internet, that bastion of information, contains nearly all one must know, and "knowledge and experience outside the digital domain becomes inaccessible, unrepresented, out of the loop" (Irvine, 1997, p. 122). But the Internet is far from containing the sum of human knowledge. In fact, the very serious limitations and challenges of Internet technology make its use as a source of reliable information a daunting intellectual exercise.

Traditional versus electronic information retrieval

Mere access to a network connection in and of itself does not make one "information rich" relative to someone who does not have such access. Any such conceptualization, as Merton (1996) makes clear, is defective "because it fails to recognize that there is nothing inherently informative about anything written, typed, spoken, drawn, or photographed. Information is something intangible that must be mined from data in any form and put to use by whoever is doing the mining. Information may be stored in written form, but that writing does not transform back into information until it is put to some use by someone" (p. 3). Within the context of American higher education, the "someone" is the undergraduate who is, or should be, trained adequately with critical-thinking skills to profitably interact with learning materials, be they lecture notes, textbooks, or website documents. In fact, interaction between learner and content is the traditional hallmark of an undergraduate education; "without it there can be no education, since it is the process of intellectually interacting with content that results in change in the learner's understanding, the learner's perspective, or the cognitive structures of the learner's mind" (Moore, 1989, p. 2).

As an aid to both access and learning, traditional sources of information in a research or academic library—books, journals, and other resources—have been organized in a central location and evaluated in a hierarchical fashion by experienced reference librarians. Specialized indexes and databases have been produced by professional and scholarly organizations that select resources for inclusion based on considerations of quality (Kirk, 1999). Such criteria may include the reputation of the author, the presence of a peer review process, internal bias, contextual awareness of scholarly literature, accuracy or verifiability of details, and currency or timeliness of information (Tillman, 1999). In brief, when students have used conventional search strategies in traditional academic libraries, the documents obtained have already been filtered for quality by information professionals. But it is not typically the case for information searches conducted on the World Wide Web.

The real strength of the World Wide Web—and a major problem in undergraduate research—resides in its nonhierarchical structure and its distributed system of information storage. The Web is a vast panoply of information, at the one end a sort of vanity press containing, as education professor Stephen Kerr colorfully describes it, "information by anyone, for anyone. There's racist stuff, bigoted, hate-group stuff, filled with paranoia; bomb recipes; how to engage in various kinds of crime, electronic and otherwise; scams and swindles. It's all there. It's all available" (Oppenheimer, 1997, p. 61). At the other end are the peer-reviewed scholarly articles, book reviews, digitized monographs, and a rapidly expanding base of electronic journals that exist without a printed counterpart. In between is an array of "gray literature," the pamphlets, technical reports, and odd pieces that once occupied what the last generation of student scholars knew as "the vertical file." Here too on the Web reside the sites of professional associations, government repositories, educational and research organizations, U.S. military branches, not-for-profit organizations, and commercial enterprises (Tillman, 1999). This list is not inclusive, but it underscores the problems of evaluation most students confront in the process of distinguishing the on-line wheat from the chaff. And this is precisely the point: "the Web's decentralization and hierarchical structure may create an illusion of equivalence among sources of content, flattening or leveling their perceived value" (Irvine, 1997, p. 123).

For many students, the inherent weaknesses of search engines and a lack of generic evaluation skills make research on the Web problematic. Internet search engines such as AltaVista, Infoseek, or Lycos retrieve information from publicly accessible Web, Gopher, and FTP servers using "spiders" and "crawlers," which are essentially robot programs that mechanically establish the relevance of sites based on the frequency of repetition of key terms. In other words, many search engines conduct *descriptive* rather than conceptually *evaluative* searches (Kirk, 1996; Tillman, 1999). More sophisticated search engines are under development, and already intermediary review and evaluation tools, such as the Lycos Top 5%, Magellan Internet Guide, and the Marr-Kirkwood Business School Rating Guide, are shaping the future of conceptual searches conducted mechanically.

One major initiative, the EDUCAUSE instructional management system (IMS), deserves special attention. IMS was organized precisely because of the lack of inherent structure or standards for accurately and fully describing available content on the World Wide Web. IMS proposes to develop a substantial body of instructional software with the express aim of overcoming three major obstacles to providing effective online materials and learning environments:

- Lack of standards for locating and operating interactive platform-independent materials.
- Lack of support for the collaborative and dynamic nature of learning.
- Lack of incentives and structure for developing and sharing content.

The fundamental intent of the project is to provide technical standards, not academic or pedagogical standards. IMS technical standards, it is claimed, will eventually support the widest possible range of pedagogical styles. Software products meeting IMS specifications are expected to reach the market in 2000. Progress on this initiative is reported at http://www.ims.imsproject.org.

No discussion of quality would be complete without addressing information technology's role in both improving communication and creating too much of it. Because it is so easy, people often communicate electronically because they can rather than because they really need to. Many distance education faculty complain of being overwhelmed by e-mail from students, even though they have designed their courses around frequent contact with students, a level of contact they would never have imagined with a traditional class. They also fail to set the rules for contact; instead, they tell students to e-mail them with *any* question. Students have lots of questions, comments, and concerns that, when expressed through e-mail, must often be answered one at a time, over and over. It is no wonder that many faculty become overwhelmed by the kind of communication made possible by the new technology.

The educational impact of Internet commercialization

The credibility of content on the Internet is further compromised by the medium's increased commercialization. The history of Internet development, like that of radio and television, is one of incremental transformation from a medium that many see as an international education resource to one that is being expropriated by commercial interests (Burbules and Callister, 1998; Coyle, 1995; Tyack and Cuban, 1995). For the moment, a delicate balance exists between two visions:

> *At one extreme is an entertainment-based model in which the principal services include video dial tone (VDT, a sort of on-line Blockbuster Video), a glorified Home Shopping Network, and other consumer-driven services designed to make spending money as easy as a phone call. At the opposite end of the spectrum of possibilities is a public-interest/educational-based model in which the principal services include distance learning projects, government information access, telecommuting or work-at-home arrangements, and other information-retrieval projects designed to increase the flow of educational and public information.* (Martin, 1996, p. 6)

Although it is unlikely that the Internet and the World Wide Web will ever wholly resemble the entertainment model, recent developments strongly suggest movement in that direction, to the detriment of students' access to reliable, noncommercially oriented information with little mass appeal.

The traditional lines between commerce and content, between advertising and objective information, begin to blur on line.

The traditional lines between commerce and content, between advertising and objective information, begin to blur on line. A large part of the problem, according to Hansell and Harmon (1999), is that users of the Internet and World Wide Web are "loath to pay any subscription fees for information on the Internet. So the money to be made is from selling products or selling ads. And users are losing interest in small rectangular banner advertisements" (p. 2). New forms of advertising have begun to cross the line between advertising and content. For example, an on-line academic journal might imbed on its website a search engine designed to retrieve its articles. Adjacent to the search box may be one for Amazon.com or Barnesandnoble.com, two prominent on-line booksellers whose engines are programmed to stimulate a commercial transaction, less to deliver a conceptually relevant title. The educational consequences are significant:

> *Not unlike television, advertisements in cyberspace turn students (or anyone, for that matter) into products. The*

site delivers the students to the advertiser, and the more hits per site, the more lucrative the relationship between the advertiser and the site provider. This commercial arrangement creates the pecuniary impetus for site providers to create popular, attractive sites—sites that will be visited often so that the advertisements can be seen. But what is the cost of this popularity? From an educational standpoint, we believe the cost is great. The price paid for the commercial relationship is the loss of specificity, depth, and the attention to subjects of limited appeal. What is lost are controversy, minority opinions, disparate views, and criticality. And what is ultimately lost is credibility. In its place stands the bland, the safe, the sensational. (Burbules and Callister, 1998, p. 5)

Perhaps the most noteworthy development commercially is the growth of web portals like snap.com, altavista.com, and so on, with their user-friendly homepages. The importance is shown by the big-name companies that own them and the astronomical sale prices for the rights to those Web entry sites. The latest incarnation is even more interesting. The portal is very simple: one simply types in a question or indicates the topic, and the search engines (for example, Ask.com., About.com) supply the answer. This system truly takes much of the thinking out of Internet use. These free-to-the-user services advertise their availability at great expense. They do not do it out of the goodness of their hearts, for there is money to be made here.

The next wave may be free Internet access. There is already free e-mail (Hotmail, Juno, MailCity, and so on) that lets individuals keep their e-mail addresses when they change Internet service providers (ISPs). Now there is even a free ISP (Netzero.com) that provides users with free access to the Internet in exchange for some access to demographic information and advertising displays on the browser. There is very little difference between these ads and the "ads" on the more popular portal sites. So, one asks, why will people pay an ISP if they can get it for free? Whether the free ISPs can offer enough customer service and reliability to be a real threat is not clear, but they will definitely help shake out the weaker ISPs.

Educators and students are not without options. One is to take full advantage of the search tools that are available at subject-specific websites, such as the Smithsonian Natural History Museum [http://nmnhwww.si.edu/nmnhweb.html], The Labyrinth: Medieval Studies Website (Georgetown University) [http://www.georgetown.edu/labyrinth], Social Sciences (WWW Virtual Library) [http://coombs.au.edu.au/wwwvl-socsci.html], Legal Information Institute (Cornell University) [http://www.law.cornell.edu/topical.html], or the index of federal legislation [http://thomas.loc.gov/]. The user must understand, of course, that the particular website includes only selected resources from which to search, not the contents of the entire Internet (Irvine, 1997).

Another option is to use the services of a for-profit website search company or professional association. For a fee, a company like Infonautics, Inc., or a professional association like the American Mathematical Society, will conduct a sophisticated search of relevant on-line materials (Tillman, 1999). The cost of such services varies considerably, from quite reasonable to extremely expensive. As a result, many instructors, working alone or by pooling resources, create their own on-line databases of useful sites for others to use and to emulate (*An Education Technology Agenda,* 1997).

A third option represents, at present, the *hope* of an option. Faster computer networks, such as the federally sponsored Next Generation Internet (NGI) or Internet 2 (also known as "Abilene") promise to contribute better tools for researchers, scholars, and students. More than 130 universities now participate in the latter project, which will connect with such existing advanced networks as the National Science Foundation's Very High Performance Backbone Network Service, or vBNS. The super-fast fiber-optic data network should hasten the development of more powerful and sophisticated data-retrieval systems and reduce the bottleneck created by a low bandwith and commercial competition ("Indiana University Is Chosen," 1998; Kiernan, 1998).

Instructional Design Considerations
The basic premise of instructional design or instructional system design (ISD) is that learning should proceed in an orderly rather than haphazard fashion and that learners' performance can be measured. The concept originated during World War II as a response to military training needs (Ehresman, 1998). Its theoretical roots can be traced

to B. F. Skinner and the psychology of learning movement in the 1950s and to the application of systems theory to instruction, first introduced by Finn and Silvern in the 1960s (Seels and Richey, 1994). It was the collaboration of Gagne and Briggs, however, in *Principles of Instructional Design* (1974) and later of Dick and Cary in *The Systematic Design of Instruction* (1979) that ISD truly flowered.

ISD is "the process of specifying the conditions for learning" (Seels and Richey, 1994, p. 30). The process is intended to identify "exactly what needs to be learned [and] the most efficient and effective manner in which it can be taught, and to design an instructional system that matches these requirements" (Eastmond and Ziegahn, 1995, p. 61). Many such design systems or models are in use today (Dick and Cary, 1985; Gagne, Briggs, and Wagner, 1992; Haynes and Dillon, 1992; Heinich, Molenda, and Russell, 1989; Romiszowski, 1981; Wagner, 1990). According to Ritchie and Hoffman (1996), instructional sequences include at least seven common elements: "motivating the learner, explaining what is to be learned, helping the learner recall previous knowledge, providing instructional material, providing guidance and feedback, testing comprehension, and providing enrichment or remediation" (p. 1).

New models of instructional design targeting adult learners working in alternative learning environments have recently been developed (Eastmond and Ziegahn, 1995; Price and Repman, 1995). These new "facilitation" models of course design, underpinned by adult learning theory, "encourage adults to be more self-directing throughout the instructional process; capitalize on their experiences, strengths, and interests; and enable them to apply whatever knowledge and skills they learn to their own problem solving or developmental task" (Eastmond and Ziegahn, 1995, p. 61).

The main design challenge facing college and university professors who move traditional courses to the Web or to other technologically mediated environments is exploiting multimedia capabilities. In the traditional classroom, lecture can be enhanced and discussion stimulated by the use of computer-based technologies. Presentation software such as Powerpoint, Astound, and WordPerfect Presenter can produce text, graphics, video, and animation. Clip-art libraries such as Corel Draw (Version 3 and up), Corel Gallery, and WordPerfect are also the source of original graphics and animation to emphasize important points in the lecture. The Internet, too, is a useful source of graphics and sound files, but creative lecturers need to be aware of evolving copyright issues.

Important design problems arise, however, when instructors move traditional courses to the new virtual environments. Faculty may choose to extend the traditional paradigm of professor-centered instruction by simply publishing a Web page with links to lectures and additional readings beyond the textbook. In such instances, "the Web will simply remain and be more universally perceived as just a nice way to publish teaching notes and make them available to students inexpensively—a modern-age photocopying machine of sorts" (Duchastel, 1997, p. 222). By failing to design novel forms of instruction based on multimedia capabilities, faculty may be missing opportunities to stimulate real improvements in students' learning and growth (Duchastel, 1997; Henke, 1997; Ritchie and Hoffman, 1996). What is worse is that a failure to restructure traditional course material to fit the features of the selected medium (text, for example, when graphic simulation is more appropriate) may result in students' learning less (Alexander, 1996).

Such a conclusion would seem to challenge the metastudies of Clark (1983) and Russell (1993), who independently reviewed several decades of media comparison studies and concluded that instructional media are not inherently superior and do not directly influence students' achievement. "The best current evidence is that media are more vehicles that deliver instruction but do not influence student achievement any more than the truck that delivers our groceries can change nutrition. . . . Only the content of the vehicle can influence achievement" (Clark, 1983, p. 445).

Russell (1983) puts a slightly different spin on the findings: "No matter how it is produced, how it is delivered, whether or not it is interactive, low-tech or high-tech, students learn equally well with each technology and learn as well as their on-campus, face-to-face counterparts even though students would rather be on campus with the instructor if that were a real choice" (p. 2).

For Clark and Russell, the proper aim of research should be teaching and learning methods and techniques; media comparison studies are essentially misguided and irrelevant.

Critics of these metastudies do agree that methods of teaching and learning are crucially important, but also that the selection of technologies is a relevant consideration. Two issues of *Educational Technology Research and Development* (1994, 42: 2 and 3) reinvigorate the debate. Ehrmann (1995) summarizes the media comparison point of view with this analogy: "There are several tools that can be used to turn a screw, but most tools can't do it, and some that can are better for the job than others" (p. 24).

The rationale for selecting and using technologies is to provide students with the support appropriate to achieve prescribed educational outcomes as well as outcomes that might otherwise be very difficult or impossible to accomplish. Kozma and Johnston (1991) and Trevitt and Williams (1997) identify various ways IT can support student learning outcomes: (1) visualize hard-to-see processes and events, (2) get students to "do it again thoughtfully" (D.I.A.T.), (3) engage students in manipulating data, or model systems, and (4) engage students in active and co-operative learning.

Visualize hard-to-see processes and events

Providing representations in multiple modalities (for example, three-dimensional, auditory, graphic, video, text) can be accomplished with computer-based demonstration and simulation. Demonstrations, which visually display phenomena, have been used for centuries to enhance instruction. Today, the truism "a picture is worth a thousand words" has been updated by computer animation techniques and graphic capabilities to read "a moving picture is worth a million words." In a virtual environment, dynamic mathematical concepts and processes are rendered visually, in some cases for the first time (Brown, 1991); art students generate rough designs for subsequent sculptures and castings (Mones-Hattal and others, 1990); and ophthalmology residents observe the origins and development of ocular disease (Brown, 1991).

Demonstrations can be enhanced further by computer simulation. For example, to show how a fire sprinkler operates, it is usually necessary to go to a special facility, set the sprinkler off and watch the water fall. In the act, the sprinkler is partially destroyed. Therefore, it must be replaced to do another demonstration. A computer simulation, on the other hand, offers a number of advantages over traditional presentations:

- Simulations have the characteristics of illustrating or collapsing or expanding time, which can focus students' attention on critical aspects that might be missed and not be repeatable in a live demonstration.
- Simulations can become "educational field trips" that allow students to "visit" sites without the time and expense of travel.
- Simulations can eliminate the risks associated with "real" situations, such as operating a commercial boiler or performing a delicate surgical procedure.

D.I.A.T.

Word processors and mathematical programs remove much of the drudgery connected with writing and computational tasks and may encourage students to regularly revise their work. At Reed College in Portland, Oregon:

> . . . students actually pressed to get a second chance to improve their work and their grade. Gradually, the texture of the curriculum in each course [changed] toward projects developed in stages—plan, draft, conversation, another draft, final version. Each stage of work was marked by rethinking, and by learning. We called this strategy "Doing It Again, Thoughtfully," or "DIATing." (Ehrmann, 1995, p. 26)

Engage students in manipulating data, information, and system models

In nearly every technical discipline, from accounting to zoology, available interactive software permits students to gain useful experience manipulating variables in simulated environments, performing secondary analyses of research data obtained on the Web from various sources such as government agencies, and using laboratory instrumentation to gain mastery of analytical techniques. Examples of interactive software include A.D.A.M. (Animated Dissection of Anatomy for Medicine), which simulates a human body with complete animated structures for simulated student dissections [http://www.adam.com]; Mathematica, which enables students to manipulate variables and change equations for the purpose of seeing dynamic graphical representations of any function; and SimCity 2000 and 3000, which allow students to study the long-term effects of human, financial, and ecological decisions made in a simulated urban environment [http://www.maxis.com/games/simcity2000/] (Mason, 1997).

Engage students in active and cooperative learning experiences

In an authentic student-centered system of instruction, the roles of student and instructor are redefined. Each student can be expected to do far more than sit back in class "listening to teachers, memorizing prepackaged assignments, and spitting out answers"; they "must talk about what they are learning, write about it, relate it to past experiences, apply it to their daily lives. They must make what they learn part of themselves" (Chickering and Gamson, 1987, p. 3). Active learning and cooperative learning, two established classroom techniques designed for virtually any kind of classroom environment, are especially well suited to the demands of the new technologically mediated environments.

Active learning, though never very precisely defined in the literature, has been aptly described as "anything that involves students in doing things and thinking about the things they are doing" (Bonwell and Eison, 1991, p. 2). Active learning techniques often produce a scenario very different from the ones associated with the traditional classroom:

- *Students are involved in more than listening.*
- *Less emphasis is placed on transmitting information and more on developing students' skills.*
- *Students are involved in higher-order thinking (analysis, synthesis, evaluation).*
- *Students are engaged in activities (e.g., reading, discussing, writing).*
- *Greater emphasis is placed on students' exploration of their own attitudes and values.* (p. 2)

The variety of today's educational technologies makes possible many of the classroom techniques recommended by proponents of active learning: impromptu writing, student-generated questioning, small-group discussion, demonstrations, simulations, role playing, games, debates, drama, and peer teaching (Bonwell and Eison, 1991). Networked classrooms, for example, may use software such as Daedalus for prewriting, discussing, and peer-reviewing student documents [www.daedalus.com].

Cooperative learning, an active learning strategy, refers to "the instructional use of small groups so that students work together to maximize their own and each other's learning" (Johnson, Johnson, and Smith, 1991, p. iii). Cooperative learning involves more than grouping students for purposes of discussion and collaborative projects. Three kinds of learning groups—formal, informal, and base—can be organized for teaching specific content, for providing a mechanism for analysis and feedback, and for continuous support and academic assistance (p. 9). Designed originally for traditional classroom settings, cooperative learning techniques can be adapted to an electronic environment through the interactive capabilities of two-way video and computer-mediated communications. Telecommunications technology makes possible synchronous (real-time) video or on-line discussion groups as well as asynchronous (delayed) exchanges through e-mail and bulletin boards.

In traditional class discussion, a few speak and some (or many) are not even listening—maybe because they are planning what they want to say or are worried about the parking meter or are just tired. Often what is said in these discussions is of little import and poorly thought out. With asynchronous communication tools, all students can be required to participate—and (when the discussion is designed correctly) to think about what has been "said" before and to respond thoughtfully. The quality of the communication is potentially as good, or better, and there is a written record for possible assessment.

Active learning and cooperative learning can provide instructors with a conceptual framework for developing various kinds of student-centered classroom activities. Professional development workshops can serve as the catalyst for facilitating the transition from a traditional lecture-oriented classroom to an electronic, highly interactive learning environment.

On-Line Assessment
The assessment movement in higher education has been driven largely by external demands for accountability from accrediting agencies, state legislatures, and business and

education consortia (Banta, 1996; Donald and Denison, 1996). Efforts to assess the quality of student learning extend to the new, technologically mediated forms of instruction (Price and Repman, 1995; Suen and Parkes, 1997; Wills and McNaught, 1996), but measuring how much and how well students are learning in these new environments raises serious issues and poses distinct challenges to traditional notions of assessment.

Assessment, like learning itself, is multidimensional and may include cognitive learning, affective behavior, and skills acquisition. Furthermore, assessment measures may be formal or informal, summative or formative, or quantitative or qualitative (Angelo and Cross, 1993). *Summative* evaluation assesses the overall effectiveness of an entire course or project after its completion. For example, a comprehensive final exam in economics would be summative. *Formative* evaluation assesses the effectiveness of a course as an ongoing process at all stages of instruction. For instance, chapter tests or writing assignments at various times during a course would be formative. To evaluate students' achievement and assign grades, instructors use *formal* assessment tools such as quizzes, exams, term papers, and lab reports. To evaluate students' learning, instructors may use *informal* techniques such as responses to questions posed or participation observed in group discussions. Within the context of formal assessment, *quantitative* measures of student learning have usually been restricted to responses that can be statistically tabulated and analyzed, such as in multiple-choice and true-false tests. To improve reliability, a large student sample is usually necessary. *Qualitative* measures, such as essay examinations and contextual problem solving, permit a wider range and depth of responses from students, often eliciting higher-order thinking skills, purposely or inadvertently. "Using qualitative methods, assessment can be 'developmental,' judging where students are in their understanding, or 'ecological,' testing students' abilities to apply knowledge in 'authentic situations.' Assessing in ways that foster 'deep' learning is important because research shows students learn what they expect will be assessed" (Pausch and Popp, 1997, p. 2).

Formal educational assessment has evolved considerably since the 1940s, when objective testing began to dominate efforts to measure student achievement (Suen and Parkes, 1997). In recent years, computer technology has contributed a number of innovations that have increased the efficiency and adaptability of such testing. These innovations include on-screen testing, item banking, and adaptive testing. On-screen testing not only eliminates the need for paper and pencil but also scores and generates reports almost instantaneously. Item banking permits the development of algorithms that can generate an indefinite number of comparable tests, thus improving security and scheduling flexibility. Adaptive testing, by contrast, employs a computer program that varies the difficulty of test items according to the level of performance by the test taker. Testing essentially stops once the test taker achieves the highest sustainable level of correct response.

For students learning and being assessed at a distance, computerized objective testing—on-screen testing, item banking, and adaptive testing—may be inappropriate, particularly when "high-stakes" decisions must be made. Unless the test can be proctored at a mutually convenient time and location, the reliability of the test results come into question and the nature of "anytime, anywhere" learning is compromised. Nevertheless, such testing may serve as a referent to identify strengths and weaknesses or to supplement formative and summative evaluation (Suen and Parkes, 1997).

Some alternative forms of assessment may prove to be more appropriate for students at a distance who are learning in technologically mediated environments. These forms include simulations, performance appraisals, learning logs or research diaries, case studies, capstone assignments where students synthesize and apply what they have learned in the particular course or in their undergraduate major, or others. Two alternative forms of assessment in particular, authentic assessment and portfolio assessment, have received much attention in the literature because of their potential to measure depth of knowledge and higher-order cognitive skills.

Authentic assessment refers to any of several techniques designed to elicit from students competencies and skills in analyzing situations or in solving problems they would likely encounter outside the classroom—at work, at home, or at leisure. In contrast, traditional assessment "relies on indirect or proxy items—efficient, simplistic substitutes from which we think valid inferences can be made about the student's performance at those valued challenges" (Wiggins, 1990, p. 26). Authentic assessment requires the application of criterion-referenced standards and the examiner's human judgment in evaluating the quality of the achievement. Students use acquired information to demonstrate the desired skills or competencies and are measured against criteria, called rubrics, which are established well in advance of assessment and made known to students. For example, students may be asked during formative or summative assessment to use acquired discipline-specific knowledge of certain major principles to solve problems in mathematics, make a historical inquiry using primary documents, conduct research in experimental psychology, or build a model structure in architecture. The rubrics or criteria used to measure learning may be discipline methods, theories, or formulas.

Because the assessment is not "norm-referenced," that is, comparisons are not made to the performance of others, the issue of reliability arises. Wiggins (1990) has suggested that our approach to assessment might usefully approximate the "exemplary system" of Great Britain, where evaluators meet regularly "to compare and balance results on their own and national tests" (p. 27). Experience with Advance Placement essay exams in this country, however, suggests that such labor-intensive efforts would be prohibitively time-consuming and expensive if attempted beyond academic departments. On the other hand, Bowers (1994) notes, "A key question is whether the costs associated with the labor-intensive scoring system would be offset by the presumed instructional gains obtained from an assessment model that rewarded a more thorough and holistic approach to instruction" (p. 3).

The portfolio is yet another promising vehicle with which to assess a student's performance and products at a distance.

For distance education, portfolio assessment appears to be the ideal approach for summative evaluation. Even though the results of the conventional objective test, computer-assisted test, essay exams, and/or authentic performance tasks in the portfolio are individually unreliable, the rating of the collective portfolio . . . can be expected to be much more reliable. In other words, through this approach, reliability is built in through the size of the sample of performance items and tests. This approach would provide the most reliable information for summative evaluation. (Suen and Parkes, 1997, p. 8)

Defina (1992) suggests that selected works may be presented in a variety of media and may be multidimensional, at least implying that students should be encouraged to exploit the multimedia potential of computer technology. Grosvenor (1993) identifies three basic portfolio models: the *showcase* model, consisting of work samples chosen by the student; the *descriptive* model, consisting of representative work with no attempt at evaluation; and the *evaluative* model, consisting of representative products that have been evaluated by well-established criteria. In high-stakes summative evaluation, the evaluative model represents the most reliable assessment tool.

The assessment of student learning is unquestionably a complex and multifaceted process made more daunting by the varied pedagogical applications of computer multimedia. Conventional paper-and-pencil objective tests, often rewarding the mere memorization of discrete bits of information, are gradually giving way to alternative instruments that address far more worthy objectives, such as obtaining relevant information, drawing inferences from data, defining problems, working cooperatively in groups, generating and evaluating creative solutions, and communicating in clear English. Assessment developers are being challenged to create, validate, and disseminate these new instruments. In the short term, the reliability of existing instruments remain less than completely satisfactory, particularly for technologically mediated environments.

The task of integrating the new technologies into the mainstream of postsecondary teaching and learning is all the more daunting because of numerous obstacles and competing interests.

Faculty Support and Development

Improving on-line content, instructional design, and assessment of student learning is, of course, a primary consideration in reforming undergraduate education. But the single most important IT issue confronting colleges and universities, according to the 1998 Campus Computing Survey, is "assisting faculty integrate technology into instruction" (Green, 1998, p. 1). The task of integrating the new technologies into the mainstream of postsecondary teaching and learning, not to mention the broader organizational culture, is all the more daunting because of numerous obstacles and competing interests, which include:

- A lack of adequate leadership at all levels of implementation (Kearsley and Lynch, 1992);

- Overt resistance from an entrenched faculty and administrative culture, 700 years in the making (Altbach, 1992);
- The deemphasis of teaching over research, especially in tenure and promotion decisions (Cartwright, 1994; Keig and Waggoner, 1994);
- An increasing number of part-time faculty (El-Khawas, 1995) without adequate technical training or support (Digranes and Digranes, 1995); and
- Inadequate start-up and ongoing funding (Krebs, 1996).

These and other obstacles illustrate Darby's (1992) contention that "the primary constraint is neither technical nor pedagogical but organizational and social in nature" (p. 195).

If theory is autobiography, as French poet Paul Valery contends, faculty espouse the status quo because it is what they know. Changing such a culture requires changing ingrained habits and behaviors. Rao and Rao (1999) suggest that assisting faculty integrate technology into instruction is a behavior-modification process comprising three ingredients: "access to resources [that] promote the desired behavior; convenience in adapting the desired behavior; and reward and recognition for following the desired behavior" (p. 22).

In reality, access is the biggest bottleneck limiting effective use of instructional technology in both physical and virtual classrooms. "Access means not only providing physical access to instructional technology, but also creating a host of supportive factors that contribute to the use of that instructional technology" (Rao and Rao, 1999, p. 24). For example, at the University of Arizona Faculty Development Center, access to instructional technology involves an "education cycle" that progresses "from awareness of our current understanding of learning and assessment, curriculum design, and instructional techniques to providing access to equipment and support personnel as part of a curriculum design and development process" (Smith, 1996, p. 11).

A major constraint impeding the smooth implementation of the "education cycle" at Arizona and elsewhere is *time*. Investing time to learn the mechanical aspects of a well-designed, well-equipped "smart" classroom is not the problem. Faculty are generally able to operate overhead projectors, televisions and videotape players, computer projectors, and other visualizing devices with a minimum of training.

But as faculty move course components or entire courses onto the Web, technology becomes increasingly the means of communication between faculty and students and among students; as a consequence, "the design of these mediating technologies becomes correspondingly important" (Hillman, Willis, and Gunawardena, 1994, p. 33).

Designing a Web-based course with such desirable technical components as e-mail, computer conferencing, active hyperlinks, threaded discussion, bulletin boards, and file sharing (graphics, video, audio, or other) normally requires intense consultation and production support services. Though a fledgling industry has sprung up to support faculty with prepackaged course management tools (WebCT, Web Course in a Box, and CyberClass, for example), an enormous investment in time is required to create or redesign a traditional class (McCollum, 1997). Citing anecdotal evidence from British Open University, Pennsylvania State University, and ten years of personal experience building computer-based materials, Boettcher (1998a) claims that it takes an average of eighteen hours of faculty time to create one hour of Web-based instruction. Given the research and scholarly demands of faculty—particularly junior faculty seeking promotion and tenure—this time investment seems untenable without substantial release time, not to mention a reconceptualization of scholarship.

A second ingredient in Rao and Rao's (1999) recipe for electronic classroom support is standardization of technology "so that content is the only variable" (p. 24). As the distinction between distance and campus-based learning blurs, both teacher and learner benefit in a number of ways from a common, consistent, and uncomplicated *interface*— the tool that serves as the point of access and the means of interaction. Theoretically, if not practically, teacher and student should move between classroom and office, dormitory and home, in one seamless web of interconnectivity. Graves (1997) offers a rationale from the support staff's point of view:

The possible combinations of computer and network hardware, operating systems, network protocols, and basic productivity software in today's commodity Internet market number in the thousands. Each combination differs from every other in subtle ways that are

*amplified when they are connected to each other on the
network. The proliferation of these systems has placed
technical support staffs in an untenable position. Even
the more focused task of configuring and supporting a
few combinations of hardware and software for a large
client base is daunting. The number of configurations
supported by any central information technology organization accordingly must be reduced and kept to a
minimum if the institution is to avoid spiraling costs
and optimize the institutional effectiveness of its current support organizations. There will always be a
need for special purchases to meet special needs, but
these exceptions and the support costs they incur must
be minimized in favor of a few standard configurations that can be the focus of both central and distributed support staffs.* (p. 50)

The final ingredient in Rao and Rao's (1999) recipe for
assisting faculty integrate technology into instruction is re-
vamping a tenure and promotion system based on research
and publication capabilities. Perhaps the most influential
voice confronting the research monolith comes from The
Carnegie Foundation for the Advancement of Teaching. In
Scholarship Reconsidered, the late Ernest Boyer (1990)
proposes a four-dimensional model of scholarship, each
element separate but interdependent: the scholarship of
discovery; the scholarship of integration; the scholarship
of application; and the scholarship of teaching. Paulsen and
Feldman (1995) report that Boyer's proposal has already
been adopted by the National Project on Institutional
Priorities and Faculty Rewards for the purpose of promoting
the reconceptualization of scholarship among various academic disciplines.

Pertinent here, however, is the *scholarship of teaching.*
For community colleges and liberal arts colleges and, in
many instances, public comprehensive universities, teaching
remains today the central mission. Even research institutions
are beginning to address the ethical—not to mention the
political—dilemma that arises when the education of large
numbers of well-prepared undergraduate students is
entrusted, at least initially, to graduate teaching assistants
("New Report Criticizes Universities," 1998). As the stock of
teachers rises, so too do the opportunities to elevate

teaching to a level of serious scholarship. For many years, Cross has promoted the role of "*classroom researcher*—one who is involved in the evaluation of his or her own teaching and learning, even as it takes place. Such a person should be trained to be a careful observer of the teaching process, to collect feedback on what and how well students learn, and to evaluate the effectiveness of instruction" (Boyer, 1990, p. 61). Restructuring the definition and scope of scholarly activity to include great teaching reaffirms the centrality of undergraduate education.

On an optimistic note, *Campus Trends* (El-Khawas, 1995) reports that many institutions are just now beginning to respond positively to Boyer's call for more balance among teaching, research, and service. In El-Khawas's survey of more than 500 colleges and universities,

> *Close to half have increased the importance of teaching in faculty evaluations. Among public research and doctoral universities, two-thirds reported such changes. About four in ten institutions now give greater importance to teaching in their hiring decisions. One-third have made changes in the criteria for promotion of faculty. About three in ten have changed the criteria for tenure. Among public research and doctoral universities, six in ten reported such changes.* (p. 20)

Faculty today are inundated with the demands of the profession—preparing and teaching classes, assisting and assessing students, conducting research and writing scholarly articles, and engaging in a variety of service-related activities. Given sufficient access to technology, adequate time to design and develop multimedia, and appropriate compensation for creating intellectual capital, faculty will continue their record of achievement and innovation, which has made American higher education the envy of the world.

Summary
The two instructional paradigms—the traditional, campus-based classroom (including interactive television and video-conferencing, which basically replicate the classroom model) and on-line, asynchronous learning networks—are well positioned to exploit the capabilities of computer-based multimedia technologies. Maintaining a high level of

instructional quality in these two environments—as well as myriad hybrids in between—is a function of course content, instructional design, assessment measures, and institutional support. For one, Internet-based resources offer faculty and students a stunning array of content in a distributed, non-hierarchical environment. Five problems are noteworthy, however. First, search engine algorithms fail to discriminate adequately between the relevant and the trivial, requiring a degree of website evaluation skill that students cannot be assumed to already possess. Second, the line between advertising and objective information is blurred as a consequence of increased commercialization of the World Wide Web. Instructional design is yet another quality issue. Design problems arise when faculty move traditional courses to learner-centered virtual environments without restructuring the presentation of materials to accommodate the paradigmatic shift. By failing to fully exploit multimedia capabilities, faculty may be missing out on opportunities to stimulate real improvements in student learning. Fourth, traditional forms of assessment may prove inadequate to reliably measure how much and how well students are actually learning in the new technology-mediated environments. Such alternative forms of assessment, such as authentic assessment and portfolio assessment, may prove only near-term solutions for students at a distance from campus. Finally, to assist faculty with integrating technology into instruction will require an institutional commitment to providing access to technology resources for faculty training, course design, and development; providing standardized configurations to ensure continuity between instructional paradigms and efficient technical support services; and providing appropriate consideration to the teaching function in tenure and promotion decisions.

CONCLUSIONS AND RECOMMENDATIONS

Colleges and universities face the triple challenge (Ehrmann, 1995, p. 24) of making higher education more accessible, more affordable, and more effective. Among the strategies proposed to achieve these objectives none are more philosophically and politically divergent than the ones offered by millennial restructuralists and incremental reformers. The magnitude of the rift between the two viewpoints is manifest over such specific issues as academic freedom, faculty oversight, promotion and tenure, the nature and extent of interaction between faculty and students, and the role of adjunct faculty. The literature, as we have seen, is replete with opinions on how these interconnected issues will affect the overriding objectives of access, cost, and effectiveness.

With academic institutions continuing to venerate the god of inertia, any quick resolution to this debate remains highly unlikely. In the present situation, the best way to achieve harmony may be to consider an analogy suggested by noted physicist Edward Teller. In a lecture to a lay audience at Pepperdine College in the late 1970s, Teller proposed an idea of Neils Bohr, drawn from quantum mechanics and applied by Teller to contemporary global problems. The principle is complementarity, which states that "one cannot get an objective and complete understanding in any situation unless one starts from two (or more) approaches that appear to be mutually exclusive" (Teller, 1981, p. 105). In atomic theory, Teller explains, an electron (or light) can be described as a particle or as a wave, with considerable justification for either theory. What is useful here is Teller's extrapolation from atomic theory to address contemporary global problems:

> *I am proposing that we learn to consider issues from two apparently contrary views at the same time and then choose the mixture that best suits the individual situation. No doubt this idea will be subject to charges of double standards and batting for one side while pitching for the other, of inconsistency and possibly even worse. Yet, just as it was necessary to adopt complementarity in atomic science to obtain understanding and simplicity, it seems equally imperative to adopt such an approach to global problems.* (p. 139)

Such an approach permits conclusions and recommendations to be made concerning issues of access, cost, and effectiveness in higher education without the necessity of declaring winners (and therefore losers).

Conclusions

1. *Successful efforts to transform American colleges and universities into more accessible, more affordable, and more effective institutions are very likely to occur quite differently from institution to institution, based on institutional mandate, mission, and vision. Given the increasing number of nontraditional adult students, it is likely that the majority of institutions will undergo some form of significant transformation.*

Millennial restructuralists and incremental reformers have distinct agendas for meeting the challenges of access, cost, and effectiveness that today confront institutions of higher education. Both agendas, however, are incomplete and would benefit from a more thorough and objective assessment of the change process.

Incremental reformers, for instance, in their zeal to preserve higher education's core values, have generally failed to articulate how the goals of reform can be achieved within the context of the residential college experience. Clearly reformers will have to develop credible arguments for and connections between "the experience of an on-campus living/learning opportunity and the development of social and cultural characteristics that add significant value to the graduates universities produce" (Hooker, 1997, p. 10). No doubt the residential collegiate experience will continue to remain a significant segment of the higher education market, but compelling arguments to ensure its long-term viability now seem essential.

Restructuralists, on the other hand, assume that nonprofit postsecondary institutions should behave just like for-profit businesses and corporations. The implicit assumption is that were it not for laggard faculty and ineffective administrators, colleges and universities might behave more like successfully restructured American businesses and corporations. Kotter (1995), however, has studied more than 100 American companies, including Bristol-Myers Squibb, Landmark Communications, General Motors, and Eastern Airlines, that have attempted to transform themselves into more competitive entities. Most were less than completely successful, and a few were utter failures. The important lesson learned from

the few companies that managed very successful transforma-
tions was that "the change process goes through a series of
phases that, in total, usually require a considerable length of
time. Skipping steps creates only the illusion of speed and
never produces a satisfying result" (p. 59).

Transformation as it applies to American colleges and
universities is subject to extensive qualification. One of the
virtues of the American system of higher education is its
diversity. Not all types of institutions, by nature or mission,
will participate in the kinds of transformation described or
promoted in restructuralist literature. Those that do successfully transform themselves are likely to do so using a road
map that is very painstakingly crafted with direct participation from all major constituent groups.

2. *In many respects colleges and universities are businesses, but in crucial respects they are not.*

Restructuralist literature is replete with corporate
discourse. Expressions such as *vision, customers, market
niche, pricing, Continuous Quality Improvement,* and *Total
Quality Management* have taken their place alongside such
familiar concepts as mission, accountability, and strategic
planning. We must occasionally remind ourselves that such
traditional business practices as standardized accounting
procedures, marketing techniques, and strategic planning
have been basic components of college and university ad-
ministrations for only a short time. Chaffee and Sherr (1992)
trace the evolution of these practices on American campuses:

> *The demand for financial accountability in the 1960s
> ushered in standard accounting measures and prac-
> tices, with leadership from the National Center for
> Higher Education Management Systems. Pressures to
> maintain enrollment in the 1970s brought the concept
> of competition and marketing—previously considered
> uncouth at best—to the ivory tower. By the early 1980s,
> the continuing struggle to maintain both enrollments
> and finances led us to strategic planning, our first
> sustained initiatives to think seriously about our
> environment, the services we render, and the need to
> anticipate the future.* (p. 2)

Fortunately, none of the gloom-and-doom scenarios
envisioned by early critics of administrative reform have

materialized. Nonetheless, a good deal of skepticism remains, particularly in the academic sphere.

The basic business analogy—expecting colleges and universities to behave exactly like businesses—breaks down, however, when we examine two significant variables: subsidization and compliance. Recent economic research, such as the report of the National Commission on the Cost of Higher Education (*Straight Talk,* 1998), makes it quite clear that the tuition of students at nonprofit institutions typically represents one-third or less of the actual costs of the education; the balance is subsidized by legislative appropriations. If enrollments rise without a corresponding increase in legislative subsidies, "either prices have to go up, or spending, hence educational quality, has to go down" (Winston, 1998, p. B6). The commission may have assumed at the outset of its study that administrative salaries, as well as the labor structure and tenure system of college faculty, would be driving up college costs, but in the final analysis, no evidence existed for such an assumption.

Another extraordinary cost driver for nonprofit institutions is compliance with federal and state regulations. No "business" is more extensively regulated in the United States than colleges and universities. The Cost Commission found that only two federal agencies—the Federal Trade Commission and the Consumer Product Safety Commission—do not regulate postsecondary institutions. Otherwise, regulations cover occupational safety, clean air and water, campus crime, affirmative action, access for disabled individuals, historic preservation, animal and human research, control of hazardous substances, and literally dozens more, generating a preliminary list in the Cost Commission's report of three single-spaced pages (Hartle, 1998). Stanford University, for instance, estimates that nearly $20 million per year (or 7.5 cents per tuition dollar) is spent on meeting compliance regulations.

Expecting colleges and universities to "behave" like businesses, without factoring in subsidization and compliance regulations as significant variables, not only obscures the facts but can lead to detrimental legislative and college board policy.

3. *The historic commitment to core values in traditional undergraduate education has wavered; the same vacilla-*

*tion threatens to undermine general education require-
ments in electronically delivered certificate and degree
programs.*

A report from the National Association of Scholars,
The Dissolution of General Education: 1914–1993 (1996),
confirms what most academics have witnessed for years:
the undergraduate curriculum lost its foundation of basic
liberal arts coursework, particularly after 1964, with a
gradual "purging from the curriculum of many of the required basic survey courses that used to familiarize students with the historical, cultural, political and scientific
foundations of their society" (quoted in "College Has
Lost," 1996, p. 2).

Within the context of technology and restructuring, it is
difficult to see any strengthening of general education requirements in technologically mediated programs. No one
would deny the importance of preparing students for a digital economy. To do otherwise would fail to serve the many
new constituencies whose aspirations have been clearly
articulated. "Without the benefits of a broader exposure to
liberal arts and experiences prior to vocational emphasis or
professional specialization, such a policy has the long-run
cost of denying students the intellectual breadth to cope
with changing job requirements or broader roles without
retraining" (Simpson, 1993, p. 18).

A tremendous opportunity exists today for higher education institutions to distinguish themselves from the myriad
proprietary colleges and for-profit corporate universities
(Wolfe, 1998). Traditional colleges and universities occupy
an honored position in our culture not just as important
sources of new knowledge but also as shapers of values,
empowering students to improve the quality of their lives
socially, morally, and economically. Now is certainly the
time for the academy to reaffirm these core values even as,
paradoxically, it reinvents itself for a world at once more
complex and competitive.

4. *Lack of Internet access results in information poverty
for several classes of individuals and creates a new class of
postsecondary institutions.*

An ever-widening digital divide between the information
haves and the have-nots threatens to exacerbate an already
well-documented trend, first evident in the 1980s, toward
greater income inequality in American society (*The State of*

Working America, 1996). This digital divide is further creating a new class of postsecondary institutions, made up principally of rural colleges and universities that lack access to high-speed Internet connections.

Presently, information poverty can be predicted on the basis of such variables as age, income, race and ethnicity, gender, previous education, geography, household type, and physical and learning disabilities. As digitized information becomes increasingly the coin of the realm during a period of extended economic recovery, the impact of information poverty poses a serious threat to social stability.

Several predominantly rural colleges and universities may require federal and state government assistance to get connected to the high-speed portion of the Internet that elite research institutions take for granted (Kiernan, 1998). If federal and state funding is not forthcoming, or other institutional measures are not taken to establish "a point of presence," a significant disparity in research quality, scholarly communication, and innovative forms of instruction is likely to occur between institutions on the cutting edge of technology and those lacking access to the NGI or Internet 2.

5. *Distance education is unlikely to effect institutional cost savings over the short or middle term.* The fiscal crisis in higher education is real. Study after study consistently demonstrates that the costs of and demand for higher education are rising at the same time state and federal appropriations are steadily declining (Breaking the Social Contract, 1997; *Straight Talk,* 1998).

Distance education is frequently seen as a way for institutions to reduce costs and at the same time increase access to higher education. Recent research suggests, however, that no quick fixes for budgetary relief from distance education are in sight ("Some Costs of Distance Learning," 1999). One study, for example, commissioned by the Arizona community college system, found that after start-up costs are amortized, Internet and interactive television—currently the two most popular modes of distance education—are cost comparable to traditional classroom delivery after three to five years. Sustained technology infrastructure investment—including adding and upgrading hardware—keeps costs high over the short and middle term. Moreover, faculty workload increases substantially. "To teach an Internet course with 20 students," according to one economic analysis, "will take

> **This digital divide is creating a new class of postsecondary institutions that lack access to high-speed Internet connections.**

an average of 13.3 hours per week, with eight hours spent teaching and 5.3 spent on advising, administering the class and providing network support" (p. 10).

As part of an overall strategic plan to increase access to the institution and provide selected courses and services that would otherwise be problematic, distance education makes fiscal sense. But to embrace distance education as a "magic bullet" for fiscal woes is nonsense.

6. *Existing evidence on the effectiveness of media-enhanced and distance education is generally inadequate because of experimental design flaws.*

A study by the Institute for Higher Education Policy, a nonpartisan research group, raises questions about the usefulness of recent research on the effectiveness of distance education (Merisotis and Phipps, 1999). The authors of the study reviewed some 300 articles and papers on distance learning and concluded that most possessed significant shortcomings. Crucial in any such study, of course, is experimental design—the use of control groups, randomly selected subjects, double-blind testing, and so forth. Two years earlier, educational psychologist Lookatch (1997) came to a similar conclusion about technologically mediated learning: "The literature on teaching technologies since the bloom of computers in the classroom in the early 1980s has yet to present a study that [is] without a fundamental [design] flaw" (p. 110). In fairness, there are few studies validating "traditional" classroom instruction either (Brown and Wack, 1999). Traditional instruction is largely done behind closed doors, for which no records exist. Technology-based instruction is far more *public* and therefore an easy target. Nevertheless, what is needed to counter charges by critics that alternative modes of delivery do not provide students with effective—much less *improved*—learning experiences are large-scale longitudinal studies undertaken by organizations, such as Educational Testing Service, that have proven expertise in such areas. Bork (1991) contends that the alternatives—small-scale studies and metanalyses of small-scale studies—misuse statistics and make sweeping and unwarranted generalizations.

7. *Containing the costs of academic and administrative computing today requires a campuswide rather than department-level perspective.*

For nearly two decades, academic and administrative computing were worlds apart in both purpose and function. Academic computing tended to serve the needs of scholars and researchers, somewhat less classroom instructors.

On the administrative side, legacy system mainframes stored student records and processed financial transactions. In recent years, computer applications for clients and servers have eclipsed legacy-based systems: "The network has taken center stage as the hub for academic and business-related services" (McCandless, 1999, p. 53).

"Enterprise computing," as the new environment is called, serves a global campus clientele, each component of which has its own vested interests in network technology developments—students in the classroom or at remote sites, faculty on campus or at home, researchers in the laboratory or in the field, scholars in the library or presenting at a conference, staff in their offices or in meetings. Containing computing costs becomes the joint responsibility of administrative and academic spheres, and new levels of collaboration and cooperation between the "two cultures" are essential to good fiscal management. Partnering on difficult issues of acquisition and allocation of technological resources must replace back-room decision making of the favored or powerful few.

Recommendations

Scholarly recommendations, like personal advice, suffer as often as benefit from accumulated biases. In this case, the biases derive not only from those inherent in the hundreds of published and unpublished sources reviewed—books, articles, conference proceedings, electronic journals, list-servs, theses and dissertations, trade publications, and more—but also from almost three decades of working with students—in both traditional and distance learning environments—instructional designers and technologists, textbook publishers and technology vendors, administrators and board members, union officials and political activists, and state representatives and community leaders, all of whom have very good reasons for pursuing very different agendas. The following recommendations reflect an educator's bias, in the form of an action agenda, and attempt to address the most pressing issues in higher education reform.

1. *Prepare to lobby more aggressively for state and federal policy reform on higher education issues.* For many

faculty and some presidents, lobbying is a dirty word and a dirty business. But as Cook (1998) explains in *Lobbying for Higher Education: How Colleges and Universities Influence Federal Policy,* without a drastic change in the way traditional higher education associations work, the G.O.P.-led 104th Congress might well have slashed federal student aid programs. In 1995, an array of higher education associations, such as the American Council on Education and the National Association of Independent Colleges and Universities, established the Alliance to Save Student Aid and used the same grassroots lobbying tactics perfected by such experienced groups as the American Association of Retired Persons (Lederman, 1998).

With a fiscal crisis looming in higher education, academe's "community of scholars" must transform itself into a *community of policy advocates.* With a steady growth in costs per student since the 1970s coupled with a decline in public funding over the same period, college and university decision makers have rightly sought to increase institutional productivity—in some cases, however, through ill-conceived and poorly planned distance education initiatives—and threatened in the process the quality of its products. Quality education—whether delivered in traditional or technologically mediated modes—cannot be purchased "on the cheap." Technology is expensive, and supporting that technology is equally expensive and continuous. Making a case for state and federal appropriations that keep pace with the costs of educating students can no longer be the exclusive domain or major responsibility of Washington-based higher education associations. Administrators *and* faculty have to begin to examine more closely the process by which their institutions in concert with other institutions can increase their effectiveness in state capitals and on Capitol Hill.

2. *Develop a reward system that places a high value on teaching and the innovative uses of technology, even when the two may prove mutually exclusive.* Undergraduate teaching has received deserved critical attention in both the popular and education media, most recently from a panel of scholars assembled by the nonprofit Carnegie Foundation for the Advancement of Teaching. The panel's report, *Reinventing Undergraduate Education: A Blueprint for America's Research Universities* (1998), chides the 125

> *Quality education—whether delivered in traditional or technologically mediated modes—cannot be purchased "on the cheap."*

research institutions in this country for shortchanging undergraduate students, particularly freshmen, who are often taught by untrained or poorly trained teaching assistants. Although the report focuses attention on our premier research universities, which constitute 3 percent of our nation's institutions of higher education, the theme of the report has major implications for the remaining 97 percent.

Faculty know implicitly that research and scholarly publication remain the surest path to promotion and tenure. As the number of faculty exploring instructional applications of computer simulations, scientific imagery, and the World Wide Web reaches critical mass, however, the current tenure and reward system must change. Teaching—and research on teaching—must be elevated to a level of serious scholarship, much as Boyer (1990) proposed in *Scholarship Reconsidered*. Already gaining national attention as a developmental and evaluative tool is the teaching portfolio, defined by Cerbin and Hutchins as "a coherent set of materials including work samples and reflective commentary on them compiled by a faculty member to represent his or her teaching practice as related to student learning and development" (Suen and Parkes, 1997, p. 2). The Ohio Board of Regents (1994) has adopted the recommendation of its Advisory Committee on Faculty Workload that puts teaching and research on a fairly equal footing: "Promotion and tenure processes, and policies for merit salary increases should be designed to reflect the reward of good teaching comparable to the reward of good research" (p. 4).

Survey data suggest that institutions are beginning to heed the call for a revamped reward system. *Campus Trends*, a survey of 500 colleges and universities, reports that

> *Close to half have increased the importance of teaching in faculty evaluations. Among public research and doctoral universities, two-thirds reported such changes. About four in ten institutions now give greater importance to teaching in their hiring decisions. One-third have made changes in the criteria for promotion of faculty. About three in ten have changed the criteria for tenure. Among public research and doctoral universities, six in ten reported such changes.* (El-Khawas, 1995, p. 20)

As the number of faculty exploring instructional applications of computer simulations, scientific imagery, and the World Wide Web reaches critical mass, the current tenure and reward system must change.

Ultimately, a focus on innovative uses of technology will challenge many of our assumptions about traditional teaching and may significantly alter the scope of scholarly activity. A resulting political rift between technologically literate faculty and traditional scholar-teachers should be anticipated as distance education assumes a larger role in most higher education institutions.

3. *Promote universal Intranet access to campus networks by standardizing hardware and software configurations.*

Fewer baseline configurations of campus hardware and software should be a cornerstone of universal Intranet access strategy (Graves, 1997). The purpose behind such a strategy is threefold: (1) to provide students, faculty, and staff with convenient, affordable, and ubiquitous access to the campus network; (2) to increase the timeliness and effectiveness of campus technical support services; and (3) to reduce the spiraling costs associated with fully supporting a wide array of hardware and software combinations. Significant equity issues and practical matters have to enter the equation as well. In the early stages of implementing universal access, many students will be unable financially or for other reasons to make a smooth transition to the new system's limitations; computer labs should be upgraded to accommodate the needs of such students. Furthermore, specialized hardware and software will always be necessary to conduct ongoing research. A sound financial plan that accommodates both the computing needs of researchers and network access requirements of students, faculty, and staff should be part of the institution's overall strategic plan.

4. *Promote universal access to the National Information Infrastructure as a vital social utility.* For most of the twentieth century, public policy initiatives to provide basic telephone services, including emergency 911 and operator-assisted services, have proven extraordinarily successful. Now, at the beginning of the new century, the concept of universal service has been expanded to include public Internet access to the National Information Infrastructure. Such access has been declared by public interest groups and others as "an essential human right, and communication and public access as a public good" (Clement and Shade, 1996, p. 2). The Rand Corporation's study on universal access to e-mail (Anderson and others, 1995) concluded that

beyond stimulating economic activity, the main objective of universal access is "achieving active responsive citizen participation in our national dialog for all citizens—participation not only in national policies but in local affairs, job markets, educational systems, health and welfare systems, international discourse, and all other aspects of society" (p. 5).

Colleges and universities are uniquely positioned to conduct research on the direct benefits of such access. One of the original efforts in this area is the Blacksburg Electronic Village, which linked Virginia Tech with the town of Blacksburg and involved partnerships among the university, political entities, and telecommunications providers. Another aspect is the existence of relatively unsophisticated free nets, such as the Naples, Florida, Free Net. This no-cost way for citizens to access the Web is the result of commercial sponsors (with less obvious involvement than the commercial portals or "free" ad-sponsored ISPs such as Netzero.com and volunteer boards). More recently, the Graduate School of Library and Information Science at the University of Illinois at Urbana-Champaign is, as of this writing, in the middle of a two-year, $1.3 million program to get low-income families in the Urbana-Champaign area involved in a virtual community designed to provide practical information resources and interactive communication options for participants (McCollum, 1997). For example, "families with health problems might benefit from information provided by a local hospital, while people on welfare could get information about public-assistance programs straight from the state government" (p. A30). The project began in January 1998 with the distribution of 1,000 personal computers to participating residents of low-income neighborhoods. The goal of this and other similar university research projects to follow will be to continue to expand our understanding of the concept of access well beyond a simple electronic network connection.

5. *Affirm the social nature of learning.* "The world does not run on information," observes Diana Oblinger. "It runs on relationships" (1998, p. 426). Networked digital communications technologies, used to the fullest advantage, create access to hypermedia resources that fuel social interaction. Part of a higher education is indeed transmission of information, as in a clearly organized and well-delivered lecture. "It is also about practice—thinking, writing, speaking, and experimenting. It is

also about human interaction—challenging, critiquing, debating, and motivating" (p. 427). Virtual learning environments, designed to support or supplant the traditional classroom, permit effective group learning that closely approximates the often unrealized potential of the traditional classroom. Some of these learning activities may include faculty- or student-led discussions, panel discussions, e-lectures, individual group presentations, formal and informal debates, and role playing (Harasim, 1997).

Efforts to reduce direct faculty participation in the learning dynamic of students—to reduce institutional costs or increase students' control of the learning process—should be reconsidered in light of social learning theories that explain how knowledge is constructed:

> *On the one hand, students shape their understanding of ideas to be more consistent with what others think if for no other reason than to make them more readily communicated. On the other hand, knowledge construction involves the social context in which information is created, learned and applied, for example the beliefs and expectations of a culture or the "culture" of a discipline, profession, or organization.* (Winn, 1997, p. 2)

Without faculty presence to "challenge learner assumptions, question their values, and encourage their explorations" (O'Banion, 1996, p. 23), learning exists in a virtual vacuum.

6. *Require of all students the generic skills of mediacy and numeracy.* One universal objective of higher education about which there is no controversy is the development of critical-thinking skills in our students that transcend subject matter divisions. Critical thinking, by definition, is "the intellectually disciplined process of actively and skillfully conceptualizing, applying, analyzing, synthesizing, and/or evaluating information gathered from, or generated by, observation, experience, reflection, reason, or communication, as a guide to belief or action" (Paul, 1995, p. 1). Both for citizen participation and for holding a job in a highly technological workplace, disciplined, self-directed thinking is more important than merely acquiring an ever-shifting knowledge base of a

specific discipline. High-performance computing has expanded the base meaning of critical thinking to include *mediacy* and *numeracy*. Mediacy refers to the ability to interpret and communicate information in multimedia format, including text, graphics, audio, and video. Mediacy is meant to contrast with "earlier notions of literacy by suggesting both the multidimensionality and the interactivity (or immediacy) of the complex digital objects that will constitute the fabric of information and communication in the near future" (Anderson and Bikson, 1998, p. 4).

Numeracy, on the other hand, refers to the ability to interpret and communicate quantitative information. Steen (1998) describes the implication of numeracy for the average American:

> *The entire federal budget is online, available for downloading and analysis by any person with access to a networked computer. So too are school board budgets, mutual fund values, and local used car prices. Every desktop computer includes spreadsheet software more powerful than programs available to professional accountants twenty years ago. No longer is the calculation of car loans or mortgage rates an esoteric specialty known only to bankers. Now all numerate citizens may determine for themselves the economic impact of their own decisions, and of the decisions their elected representatives are making on their behalf.* (p. 1)

Particularly, but not exclusively, for learning in technologically mediated environments, the critical skills of mediacy and numeracy must supplement, not supplant, traditional thinking skills.

7. *Preserve the quality and core values that undergird and distinguish higher education from corporate training, even as institutions work to untangle the knotty issues of productivity, efficiency, and effectiveness.* Before 1980, postsecondary institutions defined and measured quality in terms of "inputs"—for example, average SAT scores of successful applicants, the number of faculty possessing doctorates, or the extent of library holdings. With the 1980s came external pressures to assess outcomes, or to document "outputs," including test scores or graduation rates (Chaffee and Sherr,

Disciplined, self-directed thinking is more important than merely acquiring an ever-shifting knowledge base of a specific discipline.

1992). More recently, legislators, employers, and students have demanded that colleges and universities develop stricter measures of accountability and academic productivity.

As instructional technology and distance learning enter the mainstream of educational practice, increasing attention will be paid to quality and assessment, particularly for programs heavily dependent on telecommunications technology. Eleven western states, having already taken the unprecedented step of endorsing the concept of a virtual university to serve the entire region, are grappling with various criteria to address quality. Among the available frameworks that may assist state higher education regulatory agencies, regional accrediting associations, and higher education institutions are the "Principles of Good Practice for Electronically Offered Academic Degree and Certificate Programs" developed by the Western Cooperative for Educational Telecommunications at the Western Interstate Commission for Higher Education (Johnstone and Krauth, 1996). These principles are offered not as a formal policy statement but as a set of guidelines for institutions to follow in regulating their own electronically delivered programs.

National faculty unions have generally recommended a go-slow approach to developing electronically delivered certificate and degree programs. More recently, the American Federation of Teachers has gone on record as opposing "undergraduate degree programs taught entirely at a distance and views such programs as problematic at the graduate level also" (Task Force, 1996, p. 14). The union contends that "teaching and learning in the shared human spaces of a campus are essential to the undergraduate experience and cannot be compromised too greatly without rendering the education unacceptable" (p. 14).

Individual institutions will indeed need to move cautiously with respect to electronically delivered programs, not only because they represent such a radical departure from the known terrain of educational delivery but also because recent summative studies issued by the nonpartisan Institute for Higher Education Policy and by the College Board have raised serious concerns about quality and access as they relate directly to such programs (Blumenstyk and McCollum, 1999; Gladieux and Swail, 1999; Merisotis and Phipps, 1999).

As we move to an uncertain future, we should remind ourselves of the one constant albeit elusive goal of teaching: to produce an educated person, as defined by Steven Crow, executive director of the North Central Association's Commission on Institutions of Higher Education:

We should remind ourselves of the one constant albeit elusive goal of teaching: to produce an educated person.

We define an educated person as one capable of independent, critical thinking, about the broader social, economic, cultural, and political environments in which all of us build our individual and corporate lives. To be sure, we expect that student learning will result in achieved competence in applied skills and proven mastery of specific bodies of knowledge, but we aim at something larger. Perhaps to too large an extent, institutions of higher education have turned to the general education program to carry the responsibility of achieving this broader goal, but it appears to remain absolutely central to what we mean when we talk about higher education. We want our students to be life-long learners, impelled to continued learning by informed curiosity and equipped to be intellectually rigorous in their pursuit of knowledge. (1997, p. 491)

REFERENCES

Access Technology. (1998). "Access Technology: An Overview."
[http://www.dors.state.il.us/atec/atecover.htm]

"The Administration's Agenda for Action." (1993). Version 1.0.
[http://metalab.unc.edu/nii/NII-Agenda-for-Action.html]

"Adults with Learning Disabilities: Definitions and Issues." (1995).
National Adult Literacy and Learning Disabilities Center.
[http://novel.nifl.gov/nalld/defini.htm]

Alexander, S. (1996). "Teaching and Learning on the World Wide
Web." [http://elmo.scu.edu.sponsored/ausweb95/papers/
education2/alexander]

Allen, Henry Lee. (1997). "Tenure: Why Faculty, and the Nation,
Need It." *Thought and Action, 13,* 75–88.

Altbach, Philip G. (1992). "Patterns in Higher Education
Development: Toward the Year 2000." In *Emergent Issues in
Education: Comparative Perspectives,* edited by Robert
F. Arnove, Philip G. Altbach, and Gail P. Kelly. Albany, NY:
SUNY Press.

"Americans With Disabilities." (1991–92). Washington, DC: U. S.
Bureau of the Census. [http://www.census.gov/population/
www/pop-profie/disabil.html]

Anderson, Robert H., and Bikson, Tora K. (1998). "Focus on
Generic Skills for Information Technology Literacy." Washington,
DC: The Rand Corporation.
[http://www.rand.org/publications/P/ P8018/]

Anderson, Robert H., and others. (1995). "Universal Access to
E-Mail: Feasibility and Societal Implications." Washington, DC:
The Rand Corporation. MR-650-MF.

Angelo, Thomas A., and Cross, K. Patricia. (1993). *Classroom
Assessment Techniques: A Handbook for College Teachers.* (2nd
ed.) San Francisco, CA: Jossey-Bass.

Arsenault, MaryLou. (1997). "How to Identify and Assess the
Needs of Older Adults Related to Learning
Technologies." *Coming of Age Conference Proceedings
and Report,* March 21–23, University of Regina,
British Columbia.

Aslanian, Carol C. (1998). *Adult Learning in America: A National
Study of How, When, Why Adults Go Back to School.*
Washington, DC: The College Board.

Assuring Quality in Distance Learning: A Preliminary Review.
(1998). Washington, DC: Council for Higher Education
Accreditation.

Atkinson-Grosjean, Janet. (1998). "Illusions of Excellence and the Selling of the University: A Micro-Study." *Electronic Journal of Sociology, 3,* 1–17. [http://www.sociology.org/content/vol003.003/atkinson.html]

Austin, Ann E., and Baldwin, Roger G. (1991). *Faculty Collaboration: Enhancing the Quality of Scholarship and Teaching.* ASHE-ERIC Higher Education Report No. 7. Washington, DC: School of Education and Human Development, The George Washington University. (ED 416 805)

Baker, Kim. (1997). "Pass It On: Plan for Achieving Self-Support With Information Technology Opportunities Nationwide." Information Technology Association of America. [http://www.itrecruitermag.com/Articles/pass_it_on.html]

Banathy, Bela H. (1968). *Instructional Systems.* Palo Alto, CA: Fearon Publishers.

Banta, Trudy. (1996). *Assessment in Practice: Putting Principles to Work on College Campuses.* San Francisco, CA: Jossey-Bass.

Barker, Donald I. (1994). "A Technological Revolution in Higher Education." *Journal of Educational Technology Systems, 23,* 155–168.

Barr, Robert B., and Tagg, John. (1995). "From Teaching to Learning: A New Paradigm for Undergraduate Education." *Change, 27,* 13–25.

Bates, Anthony W. (1996). "The Impact of Technological Change on Open and Distance Learning." Keynote Address at Open Learning: Your Future Depends on It, December 4–6, Brisbane, Queensland, Australia. [http://bates.cstudies.ubc.ca/brisbane.html]

Beamish, Anne. (1996). "Background." MIT Colloquium on Advanced Technology, Low-Income Communities, and the City, February 14, Boston, MA.

Belenky, Mary Field, and others. (1986). *Women's Ways of Knowing.* New York, NY: Basic Books.

Blumenstyk, Goldie. (1997, October 31). "A Feminist Scholar Questions How Women Fare in Distance Education." *Chronicle of Higher Education,* A36.

Blumenstyk, Goldie. (1998a, July 10). "Leading Community Colleges Go National With New Distance-Learning Network." *Chronicle of Higher Education,* A16.

Blumenstyk, Goldie. (1998b, July 24). "U. of North Carolina Will Urge Students to Buy IBM Laptops." *Chronicle of Higher Education,* A20.

Blumenstyk, Goldie, and McCollum, Kelly. (1999, April 16). "2 Reports Question Utility and Accessibility in Distance Education." *Chronicle of Higher Education,* A31.

Boettcher, Judith. (1998a). "Distance Learning: How Much Does It Cost? It All Depends . . ." *Syllabus, 11,* 56–58.

Boettcher, Judith. (1998b). "Taking Off With Distance Learning: Are We There Yet?" *Syllabus, 12,* 22–26.

Bonwell, Charles C., and Eison, James A. (1991). *Active Learning: Creating Excitement in the Classroom.* ASHE-ERIC Higher Education Report No. 1. Washington, DC: Graduate School of Education and Human Development, The George Washington University. (ED 336 049)

Bork, Alfred. (1991). "Is Technology-Based Learning Effective?" *Contemporary Education, 63,* 6–14.

Bowers, Donald. (1994). "Where Are We Going with Alternative Assessment?" *Contemporary Education, 3,* 3–12.

Boyer, Ernest L. (1990). *Scholarship Reconsidered: Priorities of the Professoriate.* Princeton, NJ: The Carnegie Foundation for the Advancement of Teaching. (ED 326 149)

Breaking the Social Contract: The Fiscal Crisis in Higher Education. (1997). Washington, DC: Commission on National Investment in Higher Education. [http://www.rand.org/publications/CAE/CAE100/index.html/overview]

Brown, Gary, and Wack, Mary. (1999, May/June). "The Difference Frenzy and Matching Buckshot With Buckshot." *Critical Reading.* [http://www.horizon.unc.edu/TS/reading/1995–05.asp]

Brown, Judith. (1991). "Images for Insight: From the Research Lab to the Classroom." *Journal of Computing in Higher Education, 3,* 104–126.

Burbules, N., and Callister, T. (1998). "Paying the Piper: The Educational Cost of the Commercialization of the Internet." *Electronic Journal of Sociology, 3,* 18–30. [http://www.sociology.org/content/vol003.003/callister.html]

Campbell, Katy. (1997). "The Adult Learner—Characteristics." Edmonton, BC: Academic Technologies for Learning. [http://www.atl.ualberta.ca/presentations/learnchar/learnchar.html#part1]

Carnegie Foundation for the Advancement of Teaching. (1998). *Reinventing Undergraduate Education: a Blueprint for America's Research Universities.* Menlo Park, CA.

Cartwright, G. Philip. (1994). "Information Technology: Considerations for Tenure and Promotion." *Change, 26,* 26–28.

Cartwright, G. Philip. (1997). "Three Years and Eight Days." [http://contract.kent.edu/change/articles/julaug97.html]

Chaffee, Ellen Earle, and Sherr, Lawrence A. (1992). *Quality: Transforming Postsecondary Education.* ASHE-ERIC Higher Education Report No. 3. Washington, DC: Graduate School of Education and Human Development, The George Washington University. (ED 351 922)

Chickering, Arthur W., and Gamson, Zelda F. (1987, March). "Seven Principles for Good Practice in Undergraduate Education." *AAHE Bulletin.* (ED 282 491)

Clark, Richard. (1983). "Reconsidering Research on Learning From Media." *Review of Educational Research, 53,* 445–459.

Clement, Andrew, and Shade, Leslie Regan. (1996). "What Do We Mean By 'Universal Access'? Social Perspectives in a Canadian Context." Proceedings of INET96, June 25–28, Montreal, Quebec. [http://www.fis.utoronto.ca/research/iprp/ua/inet.html]

"College Has Lost Its General Education Anchor, Study Shows." (1996). *On Campus, 15,* 2.

Collins, Mauri P., and Berge, Zane L. (1994). "Guiding Design Principles for Interactive Teleconferencing." Paper presented at the Pathways to Change: New Directions for Distance Education and Training Conference, September 29–October 1, University of Maine at Augusta.

Collins, Mauri P., and Berge, Zane L. (1996). "Facilitating Interaction in Computer Mediated Online Courses." FSU/AECT Distance Education Conference, June, Tallahassee, FL.

"CommerceNet/Nielsen Internet Demographic Survey." (1998). CommerceNet Research Center [http://www.commerce.net/ research/stats]

Cook, Constance Ewing. (1998). *Lobbying for Higher Education: How Colleges and Universities Influence Federal Policy.* Nashville, TN: Vanderbilt University Press.

Cordes, Colleen. (1998, January 16). "As Educators Rush to Embrace Technology, A Coterie of Skeptics Seeks to Be Heard." *Chronicle of Higher Education,* A25–26.

Coyle, Karen. (1995, January 26). "Universal Access." Keynote address at Student Pugwash, Stanford University. [http://www.dla.ucop.edu/~kec/pugwash.html]

Cross, K. Patricia, and Angelo, Thomas A. (1988). *Classroom Assessment Techniques: A Handbook for Faculty.* Ann Arbor, MI: National Center for Research to Improve Postsecondary Teaching and Learning, University of Michigan. (ED 317 097)

Crow, Steven D. (1994–95). "Distance Learning: Challenges for Institutional Accreditation." *NCA Quarterly, 69,* 354–358.

Crow, Steven D. (1997). "Measuring Moving Targets: An Unfinished Theme." *NCA Quarterly, 71,* 490–491.

Cuban, Larry. (1986). *Teachers and Machines: The Classroom Use of Technology Since 1920.* New York, NY: Teachers College Press.

Cundift, Lynne, and Briscar, Sandy. (1998). "Laptops for Everyone: Changing the Way Students Learn and Colleges Do Business." *Leadership Abstracts: World Wide Web Edition, 11,* 1–5. [http://www.league.org/labs0498.html]

Curry, Barbara. (1992). *Instituting Enduring Innovations: Achieving Continuity of Change in Higher Education.* ASHE-ERIC Higher Education Report No. 7. Washington, DC: School of Education and Human Development, The George Washington University. (ED 358 809)

Daniel, Sir John S. (1996). *The Mega-Universities and the Knowledge Media.* London: Kogan Page.

Daniel, Sir John S. (1997). "Why Universities Need Technology Strategies." *Change, 29,* 10–17.

Darby, Jonathan. (1992). "The Future of Computers in Teaching and Learning." *Computers in Education, 19,* 193–199.

Defina, Allan. (1992). *Portfolio Assessment: Getting Started.* Jefferson City, MO: Scholastic, Inc.

"Defining the Technology Gap." (1998). Benton Foundation. [http://www.benton.org/Library/Low-Income/one.html]

Department of Commerce. (1995). *Falling Through the Net: A Survey of the "Have Nots" in Rural and Urban America.* Washington, DC: National Telecommunications and Information Administration. [http://www.ntia.doc.gov/ntiahome/fallingthru.html]

Department of Commerce. (1998). *Falling Through the Net II: New Data on the Digital Divide.* Washington, DC: National Telecommunications and Information Administration. [http://www.ntia.doc.gov/ntiahome/net2/falling.html]

Department of Commerce. (1999). *Falling Through the Net: Defining the Digital Divide.* Washington, DC: National Telecommunications and Information Administration [http://www.ntia.doc.gov/ntiahome/fttn99.html]

Dick, Walter, and Cary, Lou. (1979). *The Systematic Design of Instruction.* Glenview, IL: Scott, Foresman.

Dick, Walter, and Cary, Lou. (1985). *The Systematic Design of Instruction.* (2nd Ed.). Glenview, IL: Scott, Foresman.

Digest of Education Statistics. (1997). Washington, DC: National Center for Education Statistics. [http://nces.edu.gov/pubs/digest97/d97+171.html]

Digranes, Jo Lynn Autry, and Digranes, Swen H. (1995). "Current and Proposed Uses of Technology for Training Part-Time Faculty." *Community College Journal of Research and Practice, 19,* 161–169.

The Dissolution of General Education: 1914–1993. (1996). Princeton, NJ: National Association of Scholars.

Donald, Janet G., and Denison, D. Brian. (1996). "Evaluating Undergraduate Education: The Use of Broad Indicators." *Assessment and Evaluation in Higher Education, 21,* 23–39.

Dubois, Jacques H. (1997, September). "Understanding the Market for Online Courses." Phoenix, AZ: The College Board, Delivering Online Courses.

Duchastel, Philip. (1997). "A Web-Based Model for University Instruction." *Journal of Educational Technology Systems, 25,* 221–228.

Eastmond, Dan, and Ziegahn, Linda. (1995). "Instructional Design for the Online Classroom." In Berge, Zane and Collins (eds.) *Computer-Mediated Communication and the Online Classroom.* Cresskill, N.J.: Hampton Press.

An Education Technology Agenda. (1997). Washington, DC: The Benton Organization. [http://www.benton.org/Library/Schools/two.html]

Ehresman, Judy. (1998). "Distance Learning: What About Instructional Design?" League for Innovation in the Community College Conference on Information Technology, November 1–4, Miami Beach, FL.

Ehrmann, Stephen C. (1995, March/April). "Asking the Right Questions: What Does Research Tell Us About Technology and Higher Learning?" *Change,* 20–27.

El-Khawas, Elaine. (1995). *Campus Trends 1995: New Directions for Academic Programs.* Washington, DC: American Council on Education. (ED 386 089)

Environmental Scanning: Looking to the Future. (1996). Athens, GA: Center for Continuing Education, University of Georgia. [http://www.gactr.uga.edu/scanning/scandef.html]

Evans, Richard I., and Leppman, Peter. (1968). *Resistance to Innovation in Higher Education: A Social Psychological Exploration Focused on Television and the Establishment.* San Francisco, CA: Jossey-Bass.

Finney, Joni. (1997). "Educational Collaboration: The Challenge of Meeting Unprecedented Enrollment Demands." *The California Higher Education Policy Center, 5,* 1–5.

Frank, Jeffrey. (1995). *Preparing for the Information Highway: Information Technology in Canadian Homes.* Ottawa, Ontario: Statistics Canada.

Gagne, Robert M. and Briggs, Leslie, J. (1974). *Principles of Instructional Design.* New York, NY: Holt, Rinehart and Winston.

Gagne, Robert M., Briggs, Leslie J., and Wagner, Walter W. (1992). *Principles of Instructional Design.* (4th Ed.). Fort Worth, TX: Harcourt Brace Jovanovich.

Gates, Kathryn F. (1998). "Should Colleges and Universities Require Students to Own Their Own Computers?" *Cause/Effect, 21,* 1–7. [http://www.educause.edu/ir/library/html/cem9839.html]

Gatliff, Bee, and Wendel, Frederick C. (1998). "Interinstitutional Collaboration and Team Teaching." *American Journal of Distance Education, 12,* 54–63.

Gilbert, Linda, and Simpson, Edward G., Jr. (1995). "Environmental Scanning: Looking to the Future." Center for Continuing Education, The University of Georgia. [http://www.gactr.uga.edu/scanning/scandef.html]

Gladieux, Lawrence E., and Swail, Scott. (1999). *The Virtual University and Educational Opportunity: Issues of Equity and Access for the Next Generation.* Washington, DC: The College Board. [http://collegeboard.org/policy/html/virtual.html]

Gladis, Steve. (1998, June). "Let's Close Gender Gap in Information Technology." *Washington Business Journal, 22,* 1–6. [http://www.amcity.com/washington/stories/062298/focus7.html]

Goldsborough, Reid. (1998). "Avoiding Information Overload." *On Campus, 18,* 12.

Graphics, Visualization, and Usability Center. (1995). "GVU Third WWW-User Survey." Atlanta, GA: College of Computing, Georgia Institute of Technology. [http://www.gatech.edu/gvu/user_surveys/survey-04-1995/]

Graves, William H. (1996). "Why We Need Internet II." *Educom Review, 31,* 1–4.

Graves, William H. (1997). "A Framework for Universal Intranet Access." *Cause/Effect, 20,* 48–52.

Green, Kenneth C. (1998). *The 1998 National Survey of Information Technology in Higher Education.* Encino, CA: The Campus Computing Project.

Green, Kenneth C., and Gilbert, Steven W. (1995). "Great Expectations: Content, Communications, Productivity and the Role of Information Technology in Higher Education." *Change, 27*, 8–18.

Grosvenor, Laura, and others. (1993). "Taking Assessment Matters Into Our Own Hands." In *Student Portfolios*. Washington, DC: NEA Professional Library.

"The Growing Caste System in Higher Education." (1998). *On Campus, 17*, 10.

Hall, James W. (1995). "The Revolution in Electronic Technology and the Modern University." *Educom Review, 30*, 1–8.

Hall, Peter. (1996). "Changing Patterns of Cities and Low-Income Communities." [http://alberti.mit.edu/projects/colloquium/summaries/hall.html]

Hansell, Saul, and Harmon, Amy. (1999, February 26). "Caveat Emptor on the Web: Ad and Editorial Lines Blur." *New York Times on the Web*, 1–6.

Harasim, Linda M. (1997). "Interacting in Hyperspace: Developing Collaborative Learning Environments on the WWW." [http://www.umuc.edu/iuc/workshop97/harasim.html]

Hartle, Terry W. (1998, March 6). "Complex Government Rules Increase the Cost of Tuition." *Chronicle of Higher Education*, A60.

Harvey, Kay, and Dewald, Nancy. (1997). "Collaboration With Faculty in Preparing Students for the Asynchronous Classroom." Washington, DC: American Library Association. [http://www.ala.org/acrl/paperhtm/d33.html]

Haynes, K. J., and Dillon, C. (1992). "Distance Education: Learning Outcomes, Interactions, and Attitudes." *Journal of Education for Library and Information Science, 33*, 34–45.

Heinich, Robert, Molenda, Michael, and Russell, John D. (1989). *Instructional Media and the New Technologies*. New York, NY: Macmillan.

Henderson, Cathy. (1995). *College Freshmen with Disabilities: A Statistical Profile*. Washington, DC: American Council on Education.

Henke, Harold. (1997). "Evaluating Web-Based Instruction Design." [http://scis.nova.edu/~henkeh/story1.html]

"High Tech Adds to High Cost of College for Grads." (1998, May 11). *Education Market News*. [wyaiwyg://8/http://www.schooldata.com/pr11.html]

Hill, Susan. (1997). "Science and Engineering Bachelor's Degrees Awarded to Women Increase Overall but Decline

in Several Fields." Division of Science Resource Studies:
Data Brief. Washington, DC: National Science Foundation
(NSF 97-326)

Hillman, Daniel C., Willis, Deborah J., and Gunawardena, Charlotte
N. (1994). "Learner-Interface Interaction in Distance Education:
An Extension of Contemporary Models and Strategies for
Practitioners." *American Journal of Distance Education, 8,*
30–42.

Hilton-Chalfee, Danny, and Castorina, Carmela. (1991). "Equal
Access to Software for Instruction—EASI." California State
University at Northridge. CSUN 1991 Annual Conference on
Technology and Persons with Disabilities. [http://www.rit.edu/
~easi/pubs/ezhist.html]

Holleque, Kathryn, and Cartwright, G. Philip. (1997). "Assessing the
Notebook Initiative."
[http://contract.kent.edu/change/articles/novdec97.html]

Hooker, Michael. (1997). "The Transformation of Higher
Education." In *The Learning Revolution,* edited by Diane
Oblinger and Sean C. Rush. Bolton, MA: Ankar Publishing
Company, Inc.
[http://horizon.unc.edu/projects/seminars/Hooker.asp]

Hopper, David H. (1991). *Technology, Theology, and the Idea of
Progress.* Louisville, KY: Westminster/John Knox Press.

"Indiana University Is Chosen to Run Nerve Center for Internet 2."
(1998, August 14). *Chronicle of Higher Education,* A23.

Information Technology Association of America. (1998). *ITAA
Report: Building the 21st Century Information Technology
Workforce.* [http://www.itaa.org/workforce/studies/recruit.htm]

Irvine, Martin. (1997). *Web Works.* New York: W. W. Norton.

Jacobs, Alan. (1995). "The Costs of Computer Technology."
Community College Journal, 66, 34–37.

James, L. R., James, L. R., and Ashe, D. K. (1990). "The Meaning of
Organizations: The Role of Cognition and Values." In
Organizational Climate and Culture, edited by Benjamin
Schneider. San Francisco, CA: Jossey-Bass.

Jewett, Frank. (1999). "Case Studies in Evaluating the Benefits and
Costs of Mediated Instruction and Distributed Learning."
[http://calstate.edu/special_projects]

Johnson, David W., Johnson, Roger T., and Smith, Karl A. (1991).
*Cooperative Learning: Increasing College Faculty Instructional
Productivity.* ASHE-ERIC Higher Education Report No. 4.
Washington, DC: School of Education and Human Development,
The George Washington University. (ED 343 465)

Johnstone, Sally M., and Krauth, Barbara. (1996). "The Virtual University: Principles of Good Practice." *Change, 28,* 38–41.

Karelis, Charles. (1999). "Education Technology and Cost Control: Four Models." *Syllabus, 12,* 20–28.

Kearsley, Greg, and Lynch, William. (1992). "Educational Leadership in the Age of Technology: The New Skills." *Journal of Research on Computing and Education, 25,* 50–60.

Keig, Larry, and Wagoner, Michael D. (1994). *Collaborative Peer Review: The Role of Faculty in Improving College Teaching.* ASHE-ERIC Higher Education Report No. 2. Washington, DC: School of Education and Human Development, The George Washington University. (ED 378 925).

Keller, James. (1995). "Public Access Issues: An Introduction." In *Public Access to the Internet,* edited by Brian Kahin and James Keller. Cambridge, MA: MIT Press.

Kiernan, Vincent. (1998, October 23). "Will the Next Generation Internet Create a New Class of 'Have-Not' Universities?" *Chronicle of Higher Education,* A23–24.

King, Donald A. (1997, June 3). "Coming of Age: The Virtual Older Adult Learner." Canadian Association for University Continuing Adult Education. Saskatoon, Saskatchewan. [http://www.crm.mb.ca/scip/oalt/projovrvue.html]

Kirk, Elizabeth. (1999). "Evaluating Information Found on the Internet." [http://milton.mse.jhu.edu:8001/research/education/net.html]

Kline, Gil. (1998). "New National Report: Benefits of a College Education Have Far-Reaching Effects." News release. Washington, DC: Institute for Higher Education Policy. [http://www.ihep.com/PR6.html]

Kornblum, Janet. (1997, March 14). "Society's Digital Divide." C/Net. [http://www.news.com/News/Item/0,4,8834.00html]

Kotter, John P. (1995, March/April). "Why Transformation Efforts Fail." *Harvard Business Review,* 59–67.

Kozma, R. B., and Johnston, J. (1991). "The Technological Revolution Comes to the Classroom." *Change, 23,* 10–23.

Krebs, Arlene. (1996). *The Distance Learning Funding Sourcebook.* (3rd Ed.). Dubuque, IA: Kendall/Hunt.

Kurfiss, Joanne Gain. (1988). *Critical Thinking: Theory, Research, Practice, and Possibilities.* ASHE-ERIC Higher Education Report No. 2. Washington, DC: School of Education and Human Development, The George Washington University.

Kurfiss, Joanne Gain. (1989). "Critical Thinking by Design." [http://www.cstudies.ubc.ca/facdev/services/newsletter/89/nov89-S2.html]

Leach, Karen, and Smallen, David. (1998). "What Do Information Technology Support Services Really Cost?" *Cause/Effect, 21,* 38–45.

Lederman, Douglas. (1998, July 10). "A Scholar Examines the Higher-Education Lobby." *Chronicle of Higher Education,* A25.

Lee, Andrea J., and Marsh, Tracy G. (1998). "Joint Ventures in Distance Education: Mapping Uncharted Terrain." *American Journal of Distance Education, 12,* 44–53.

Leyser, Y. (1989). "A Survey of Faculty Attitudes and Accommodations for Students With Disabilities." *Journal of Postsecondary Education and Disability, 7,* 97–108.

Lipton, Beth. (1998, August 20). "Digital Divide an Income Gap." C/Net. [http://www.news.com/News/Item/0,4,25470,00.html?st.cn.nws.r/.ne]

Lissner, L. Scott. (1997). "Technological Access and the Law." [http://www.isc.rit.edu/~easi/itdl/itduv.02n3/lissner.html]

Lookatch, Richard P. (1997). "Multimedia Improved Learning— Apples, Oranges, and the Type I Error." *Contemporary Education, 68,* 110–113.

Lucas, Timothy. (1998). "Educatiors Go Back to School This Fall with UCLA Extension and OnlineLearning.net," *Business Wire, 5,* 14–16.

Lunenburg, Fred C. (1998). "Constructivism and Technology: Instructional Designs for Successful Education Reform." *Journal of Instructional Psychology, 25,* 75–81.

Lynd, Robert Staughton. (1939). *Knowledge for What: The Place of Social Science in American Culture.* Princeton, NJ: Princeton University Press.

Macavinta, Courtney. (1998, May 5). "Netizens Ponder Universal Access." C/Net. [http://www.news.com/News/Item/0,4,21817,00.html?st.ne.ni.rel]

Markwood, Richard A., and Johnstone, Sally. (Eds.). (1994). *New Pathways to a Degree: Seven Technology Stories.* Boulder, CO: Western Interstate Commission for Higher Education.

Martin, Brennon. (1996). "Universal Service and Information Poverty: A New Look at an Old Problem." [http://weber.u.washington.edu/~brennon/html/papers/tis96.html]

Mason, Dave. (1997). "Education Uses of Information Technology." [http://online.anu.edu.au/CEDAMeuit.html]

Matthews, P., and others. (1987). "Faculty Attitude Toward Accommodations for College Students With Learning Disabilities." *Learning Disability Focus, 3,* 46–52.

McCandless, Glen. (1999). "Columnist's Note: What Is Enterprise Computing?" *Syllabus, 12,* 53.

McCollum, Kelly. (1997, December 12). "U. of Illinois Project Gives Poor People Computers, and Studies How They Use Them." *Chronicle of Higher Education,* A30.

McManus, Thomas Fox. (1995). "Special Considerations for Designing Internet Based Instruction." [http://ccwf.cc.utexas.edu/~mcmanus/special.html]

Merisotis, James, and Phipps, Ronald. (1999). *What's the Difference?* Washington, DC: The Institute for Higher Education Policy. [http://www.ihep.com]

Merton, Robert K. (1996). "The Dialectic of Knowledge in Production." *Electronic Journal of Sociology, 2,* 3–15.

Monaghan, Peter. (1998, June 19). "U. of Washington Professors Decry Governor's Visions for Technology." *Chronicle of Higher Education,* A23–24.

Mones-Hattal, B., and others. (1990). "Guidelines for Curricula in Computer Graphics in the Visual Arts." *Computer Graphics, 24,* 78–113.

Moore, Michael. (1989). *Effects of Distance Learning: A Summary of the Literature.* Report prepared for the Office of Technology Assessment, Congress of the United States. Washington, DC: U. S. Government Printing Office.

National Adult Literacy and Learning Disabilities Center. (1998). "Adults With Learning Disabilities: Definitions and Issues." [http://novel.nifl.gov/nalld/definiti.htm]

National Center for Education Statistics. (1997). *1996 Educational Forecast.* Washington, DC: U. S. Department of Education. [http://www.nces.edu]

"New National Report: Benefits of a College Education Have Far-Reaching Effects." (1998). Washington, DC: Institute for Higher Education Policy. [http://ihep.com/PR6.html]

"New Report Criticizes Universities." (1998). Washington, DC: Associated Press. [http://wire.ap.org/APnews/center_story.html]

Nicholson, Bobbi. (1997). "Inconspicuous Inequities: The Myth of Universal Access." *Computers in the Social Sciences, 5,* 1–7. [http://cssjournal.com/nicholso.html]

Noble, David. (1998). "Selling Academe to the Technology Industry." *Thought and Action, 14,* 29–40.

North Central Regional Technology in Education Consortium. (1997). "What Is Your Vision of Learning?" [http://www.ncrtec.org/capacity/guidewww/vision.html]

Novak, Thomas P., and Hoffman, Donna L. (1998). "Bridging the Digital Divide: The Impact of Race on Computer Access and Internet Use." [http://www2000.oggm.vanderbilt.edu/papers/race/science.html]

O'Banion, Terry. (1996, December/January). "A Learning College for the 21st Century." *Community College Journal,* 18–23.

Oberlin, John L. (1996a). "The Financial Mythology of Information Technology: Developing a New Game Plan." *Cause/Effect, 19,* 10–17.

Oberlin, John L. (1996b). "The Financial Mythology of Information Technology: The New Economics." *Cause/Effect, 19,* 21–29.

Oblinger, Diana G. (1998). "Technology and Change: Impossible to Resist." *NCA Quarterly, 72,* 417–431.

Office of Technology Assessment. (1995). *The Technological Reshaping of Metropolitan America.* OTA-ET1-643. Washington, DC: Government Printing Office.

Ohio Board of Regents. (1994). "Shifting the Culture for Student Learning: The Evaluation and Reward of Teaching." [www.regents.state.oh.us/plandocs/teaching.html]

"On Line." (1998, July 10). *Chronicle of Higher Education,* A16.

Oppenheimer, Todd. (1997, July). "The Computer Delusion." *Atlantic Monthly,* 45–64.

Paul, Richard. (1995). "Three Definitions of Critical Thinking." Santa Rosa, CA: The Center and Foundation for Critical Thinking. [http:www.sonoma.edu/CThink/definect,html]

Paulsen, Michael B., and Feldman, Kenneth A. (1995). "Toward a Reconceptualization of Scholarship: A Human Action System with Functional Imperatives." *Journal of Higher Education, 66,* 615–40.

Pausch, Lois M., and Popp, Mary Pagliero. (1997). "Assessment of Information Literacy: Lessons From the Higher Education Assessment Movement." American Library Association [http://www.ala.org/acrl/paperht./d30.html]

Pretzer, William S. (1997). "Technology Education and the Search for Truth, Beauty and Love." *Journal of Technology Education, 8,* 1–13. [http://borg.lib.vt.edu/ejournals/JTE/jte-v8n2/pretzer.jte-v8n2.html]

Price, Robert V., and Repman, Judi. (1995). "Instructional Design for College-Level Courses Using Interactive Television." *Journal of Educational Technology Systems, 23,* 251–263.

Principles of Good Practice for Electronically Offered Academic Degree and Certificate Programs. (1996). Western Cooperative for Educational Telecommunications. [http://www.wiche.edu/telecom/principles.htm]

Quality Assurance and Distance Education: Conference Summary.
(1998, May 2). Phoenix, AZ.
http://www.chea.org/Events/QA_summary.html]

Quarterman, John S., and Smoot, Carl-Mitchell. (1995, May). "Is the
Internet All Male?" *Matrix News,* 5.

"Rand Corp. Study Finds Gap Growing Between Rich and Poor."
(1996, March 20). *Source: News and Reports.*
[http://sddt.com/files/librarywire/96wireheadlines/03_96/DN96_
3_20/DN96_03_20cn.html]

Rao, Pal V., and Rao, Laura M. (1999). "Strategies That Support
Instructional Technologies." *Syllabus, 12,* 22–24.

Repman, Judi, and Logan, Suzanne. (1996, November/December).
"Interactions at a Distance: Possible Barriers and Collaborative
Solutions." *TechTrends,* 35–38.

Ringle, Martin D. (1997). "Forecasting Financial Priorities for
Technology." *Cause/Effect, 20,* 22–29.

Ringle, Martin, and Updegrove, Daniel. (1998). "Is Strategic
Planning an Oxymoron?" *Cause/Effect, 21,* 18–23.

Ritchie, Donn C., and Hoffman, Bob. (1996). "Rationale for Web-
Based Instruction." San Diego, CA: San Diego State University.
[http://edweb.sdsu.edu/clrit/learningtree/DCD/
WWWInstrdesign/Rationale.html]

Roberts, Peter. (1998). "Rereading Lyotard: Knowledge,
Commodification and Higher Education." *Electronic Journal of
Sociology, 3,* 1–16.
[http://www.sociology.org/content/vol003.003/roberts.html]

Robinson, James A. (1997). "Anti-Technology Revolution?"
[http://highwire.stanford.edu/nimr/thesis/html/node19.html]

Robinson, James A. (1997). "Anti-technology Revolution?"
[http://highwire.stanford.edu/nimr/thesis/html/node19.html]

Rockman, Saul. (1991). "Telecommunications and Restructuring:
Supporting Change or Creating It?" In *Education Policy and
Telecommunications Technologies.* Washington, DC: U. S.
Department of Education, Office of Educational Research and
Improvement.

Romiszowski, Alex J. (1981). *Designing Instructional Systems:
Decision Making in Course Planning and Curriculum Design.*
New York, NY: Nichols.

Rothenberg, David. (1997, August 15). "How the Web Destroys the
Quality of Students' Research Papers." *Chronicle of Higher
Education,* A44.

Rowlandson, John. (1997). "Making Links Between Computer Use
and Health Care Needs of Older Adults." *Coming of Age*

Conference Proceedings and Report, March 21–23, University of Regina, British Columbia. [http://www.crm.mb.ca/scip/oalt/reports/coafinalrpt.html#ka]

Rudenstine, Neil L. (1997, February 21). "The Internet and Education: A Close Fit." *Chronicle of Higher Education,* A48.

Ruppert, Sandra S. (1997). *Going the Distance: State Legislative Leaders Talk About Higher Education and Technology.* Washington, DC: National Education Association.

Russell, Thomas L. (1983). *The "No Significant Difference" Phenomenon as Reported in Research Reports, Summaries, and Papers.* Raleigh, NC: Office of Instructional Telecommunications, North Carolina State University.

Saettler, L. Paul. (1968). *A History of Instructional Technology.* New York, NY: McGraw-Hill.

Saettler, L. Paul. (1990). *The Evolution of American Educational Technology.* Englewood, CO: Libraries Unlimited.

Schön, Donald, Sanyal, Bish, and Mitchell, William J. (eds.). (1998). *High Technology and Low-Income Communities: Prospects for the Positive Use of Advanced Information Technology.* Cambridge, MA: MIT Press.

Scott, Sally S. (1997). "Accommodating College Students With Learning Disabilities: How Much Is Enough?" *Innovative Higher Education, 22,* 85–99.

Seels, Barbara B., and Richey, Rita C. (1994). *Instructional Technology: The Definition and Domains of the Field.* Washington, DC: Association for Educational Communications and Technology.

Shade, Leslie Regan. (1993). "Gender Issues in Computer Networking." Address at Community Networking: The International Free-Net Conference, August 17–19, Carleton University, Ottawa, Canada. [http://cpsr.org/cpsr/gender/leslie_regan_shade.txt]

Silver, Patricia, Bourke, Andrew, and Strehorn, K. C. (1998). "Universal Instructional Design in Higher Education: An Approach for Inclusion." *Equity and Excellence in Education, 31,* 47–51.

Simpson, William B. (1993). "Higher Education's Role in a New Beginning." *Academe, 78,* 17–19.

Smith, Karen L. (1996). "Preparing Faculty for Instructional Technology: From Education to Development to Creative Independence." CAUSE Annual Conference, Boulder, CO. [http://www.trican.com/preparin.htm]

"Some Costs of Distance Learning." (1999). *On Campus, 18,* 10.

The State of Working America, 1996–97. (1996). Washington, DC:
Economic Policy Institute. [http://epn.org/epi/epswa-ex.html]

Steen, Lynn Arthur. (1998). "Why Numbers Count." Washington,
DC: The College Board.
[http:www.collegeboard.org/index_this/firstlook/wnc/
html/wnc_pre.html]

Straight Talk About College Costs and Prices. (1998). Washington,
DC: American Council on Education.

Suen, Hoi K., and Parkes, Jay. (1997). "Challenges and
Opportunities in Distance Education Evaluation." College Park,
PA: Pennsylvania State University.
[http://www.music.ecu.edu/DistEd/EVALUATION.html]

Sullivan, Patrick. (1998). "Gender Issues in the Online Classroom."
TCC '98 Papers.
[http://leahi.kcc.hawaii.edu/org/tcon98/paper/sullivan.html]

Tapscott, Don. (1995). *The Digital Economy: Promise and Peril in
the Age of Networked Intelligence.* New York, NY: McGraw-Hill.

Tapscott, Don, and Caston, Art. (1993). *Paradigm Shift: The New
Promise of Information Technology.* New York, NY: McGraw-
Hill.

Task Force on Technology in Higher Education. (1996). *Teaming
Up with Technology: How Unions Can Harness the Technology
Revolution on Campus.* Washington, DC: American Federation of
Teachers.

Taylor, J. C. (1994). "Technology, Distance Education and the
Tyranny of Proximity." *Higher Education Management, 6,*
179–190.

Teller, Edward. (1981). *The Pursuit of Simplicity.* Malibu, CA:
Pepperdine University Press.

"Three Definitions of Critical Thinking." (1995). Santa Rosa, CA:
The Center and Foundation for Critical Thinking.
[http://www.sonoma.edu/CThink/definect.html]

Tillman, Hope N. (1999). "Evaluating Quality on the Net." Babson
Park, MA: Babson College.
[http://www.tiac.net/users/hope/findqual.html]

Trevitt, Chris, and Williams, Robert. (1997). "A List of Some
Different Types of Educational Applications Which Use
Computer and Communications Technology."
[http://online.anu.edu.au/CEDAM/edapplns.html]

Tucker, Robert W. (1995). "The Virtual Classroom: Quality and
Assessment." *Syllabus, 9,* 48–51.

Twigg, Carol. (1994a, July/August). "National Learning
Infrastructure, Part 1." *Educom Review,* 1–4.

Twigg, Carol. (1994b, September/October). "National Learning Infrastructure, Part 2." *Educom Review,* 1–5.

Twigg, Carol. (1994c, November/December). "National Learning Infrastructure, Part 3." *Educom Review,* 1–5.

Tyack, David, and Cuban, Larry. (1995). *Tinkering Toward Utopia.* Cambridge, MA: Harvard University Press.

"Universal Service: A Century of Commitment." (1998). Washington, DC: The Benton Organization.

Vasquez, Laurie. (1999). "Tips on Accessibility: Universal Design and the Web." *Tips News, 3,* 4–5. [http://video.4c.net/TIPS/newsletter/downloads/5–99.pdf]

Wagner, Ellen D. (1990). "Looking at Distance Education Through an Education Technologist's Eyes." *American Journal of Distance Education, 4,* 13–28.

"When Students Have Learning Disabilities." (1998, July 24). *Chronicle of Higher Education,* A8.

Wiggins, Grant. (1990). "Authentic Assessment: Creating Tests Worth Taking." *Educational Leadership, 49,* 26–33.

Wight, J. D. (1997). "Race and the Net: Virtual Ghetto or Non-Issue?" [http://marketspace.altavista.digital.com/.~School.asp?/showContent=yesandArticleId=397]

Willis, Barry. (1995). "Evaluation for Distance Educators." College of Engineering, University of Idaho. [http:www.uidaho.edu/evo/dist4.html]

Wills, Sandra, and McNaught, Carmel. (1996, Spring). "Evaluation of Computer-Based Learning in Higher Education." *Journal of Computing in Higher Education,* 106–128.

Wingspread Group on Higher Education. (1993). *An American Imperative: Higher Expectations for Higher Education.* Racine, WI: The Johnson Foundation.

Winn, William. (1997). "Learning in Hyperspace." [http://www.umuc.edu/iuc/workshop97/winn.html]

Winston, Gordon. (1998, March 27). "Economic Research Now Shows That Higher Education Is Not Just Another Business." *Chronicle of Higher Education,* B6.

Wolfe, Alan. (1998, December 4). "How a For-Profit University Can Be Invaluable to the Traditional Liberal Arts." *Chronicle of Higher Education,* B4.

Woody, Todd. (1998, June 28). "Higher Earning: The Fight to Control the Academy's Intellectual Capital." *Industry Standard,* 1–4. http://www.thestandard.com/articles/display/0,1449,874,00.html]

Young, Jeffrey R. (1997a, June 13). "More Colleges Charge a Separate Fee for Technology." *Chronicle of Higher Education,* A23.

Young, Jeffrey R. (1997b, October 3). "Rethinking the Role of the Professor in an Age of High-Tech Tools." *Chronicle of Higher Education,* A26–A28.

Zemsky, Robert, Shaman, Susan, and Iannozzi, Maria. (1997, November/December). "In Search of Strategic Perspective: A Tool for Mapping the Market in Postsecondary Education." *Change,* 23–36.

INDEX

Curriculum design: faculty-based reforms in, 11–12; mandatory requirements in, 5; multimedia in, 71–72; student project process in, 74

Curry, B., 18

D

Daedalus, 76

Darby, J., 81

Deferred maintenance, 21

Defina, A., 80

"Defining the Technology Gap," 32–33

Degree programs, electronically delivered, 101

Denison, D. B., 77

Department of Commerce, 24, 26, 29, 34, 35, 41

Dewald, N., 48

Dick, W., 3, 71

Digest for Education Statistics, 31

Digranes, J.L.A., 81

Digranes, S. H., 81

Dillon, C., 71

Disintermediation, 9

Dissolution of General Education, 5, 91

Distance education, 6–7, 101–2; assessment of, 78–80; institutional fiscal crisis and, 92–93; quality and effectiveness of, 93–94

Donald, J. G., 77

Dorris, A., 1

Downes, S., 63

Dubois, J. H., 26

Duchastel, P., 72

E

Eastmond, D., 71

Economic inequality, and information access, 27–29, 33, 34, 41

Economy, knowledge-based, 7–8

Education Technology Agenda, An, 70

Educational Technology Research and Development, 73

EDUCAUSE instructional management system (IMS), 66–67

Ehresman, J., 70

Ehrmann, S. C., 18–19, 47, 73, 74, 87

Eison, J. A., 75

El-Khawas, E., 81, 84, 97

E-mail communications, 67, 76, 98

Enterprise computing, 94

Environmental scanning, 45

Evaluation, summative versus formative, 77

Evans, R. I., 1

F

Feldman, K. A., 83

Faculty: as classroom researcher, 84; e-mail communications and, 67; reductions in, 9–10; research and publication capabilities of, 83; reward system, 95–96; roles, restructuralism and, 9–10; teaching-research-service roles of, 83–84; technology implementation and, 80–84; tenure erosion and, 9, 10, 14–15

Fiber Distributed Data Interface (FDDI), 54

Financial aid, federal/state: and distance education, 7; erosion of, 41

Finney, J., 21, 50

Fiscal planning: common vision in, 46–47; institutional mission and, 43; interinstitutional collaboration in, 48–52; intrainstitutional collaboration in, 47–48; leadership role in, 44; and target market reconceptualization, 45–46

Frank, J., 28

G

Gamson, Z. F., 75

Gates, K. F., 59, 60

Gatliff, B., 47, 50

Gender, universal access and, 31–32

Gladieux, L. E., 24, 41

Gladis, S., 31

Graphics, Visualization, and Usability Center, 32

Graves, W. H., 24, 82, 97

Green, K. C., 11, 59, 80

Grosvenor, L., 80

"Growing Caste System in Higher Education, The," 14

Gunawardena, C. N., 82

H

Hall, J., 6–7

Hansell, S., 68

Harasim, L. M., 99

Harmon, A., 68

Hartle, T. W., 90

Harvey, K., 48

Haynes, K. J., 71

Heinich, R. 71

Henderson, C., 36

Henke, H., 72

Heterick, R., 7

"High Tech Adds to High Cost," 42, 59

Higher education: corporate discourse in, 12, 89–91; general education requirements and core values in, 91, 100; information infrastructure project and, 23–25; lobbying, 95; and private sector

collaboration, 52–53; public social benefits of, 12–13; regulation of, 90–91; universal access to, 21–22
Hillman, D. C., 82
Hilton-Chalfee, D., 35, 37
Hoffman, B., 71, 72
Hoffman, D. L., 29, 32
Holleque, G. P., 59, 60
Hooker, M., 7–8, 13, 52, 88
Hopper, D., 5
Hybridization, 11

I

Iannozzi, M., 45–46
Information, expanded concept of, 22
Information infrastructure: higher education and, 23–25; national project, 22–23, 24, 97–98
Information retrieval, traditional versus electronic, 65–66
Information Technology Association of America, 31
Instructional reform: faculty-based, 11–12; hybridizing model of, 10–18; incremental, 10–18, 88; principle of complementarity and, 87–88; restructuralism and, 4–10, 88–89
Instructional system design, 70–76; for adult learners, 71; multimedia capabilities in, 71–72
Instructional technology: commercialization of, 67–70; communication role of, 67; and federal funding, 2, 7; historic perspective on, 1–4; obstacles to integration of, 80–81; policy implications and recommendations, 94–102; politics of, 4–18; public discourse on, 1; scale barriers in, 42; terminology, 63; theory, 3; and time constraints, 81–82; and undergraduate research, 65–66. *See also* Technology costs; Technology quality
Interactive software, 74–75
Internet: commercialization of, 67–70; content credibility of, 64–65; service providers (ISPs), 69; universal access to, 24–25
Internet 2 ("Abilene"), 70
Intranet access, 23–24, 97–98
Irvine, M., 64, 66, 70
Item banking, 78

J

Jacobs, A., 56
James, L. R., 44
Jewett, F., 41
Johnson, D. W., 76
Johnson, R. T., 76
Johnston, J., 73
Johnstone, S. M., 101

K

L

M

Mission, institutional: reconceptualization of, 44–45; and technological mission creep, 43
Mitchell, W. J., 28
Molenda, M., 71
Monaghan, P., 52
Mones–Hattal, B., 73
Moore, M., 65
Multimedia, and course design, 71–72

N

National Adult Literacy and Learning Disabilities Center, 38
National Center for Educational Statistics, 25
National Information Infrastructure (NII) project, 22–23, 24, 97–98
"New Report Criticizes Universities," 83
Next Generation Internet (NGI), 70
Noble, D., 4, 52
North Central Regional Technology in Education Consortium, 46
Novak, T. P., 29, 32
Numeracy, defined, 100

O

O'Banion, T., 9–10, 99
Oberlin, J. L., 53, 56, 57
Oblinger, D. G., 9, 98
Office of Technology Assessment, 34
OnlineLearning.net, 52
On-screen testing, 78
Oppenheimer, T., 66
Outcomes-based pedagogy, 8
Outcomes-based standards, 7

P

Parkes, J., 77, 78, 79, 96
Paul, R., 100
Paulsen, M. B., 83
Pausch, L. M., 77
Phipps, R., 93
Physical disabilities, information access and, 35–37
Politics, and instructional technology, 4–18
Popp, M. P., 77
Portfolio assessment, 78, 79–80
Price, R. V., 71, 77
Principles of Instructional Design, 71
Private sector, collaborations with, 52–53

Q

Quality Assurance, 64
Quarterman, J. S., 32

Student technology fees, 58–61
Suen, H. K., 77, 78, 79, 96
Swail, S., 24, 25, 41
Systematic Design of Instruction, The, 71
Systems thinking, 3

T

Tagg, J., 9
Tapscott, D., 55
Task Force on Technology in Higher Education, 101
Taylor, J. C., 7
Teaching function: scholarship of teaching concept and, 83–84; virtualization of, 47–48
Team teaching, technologically mediated, 49–50
Teaming Up With Technology, 53
Technological humanism, 11
Technological minimalism, 18
Technology collaborations: interinstitutional, 48–52; intrainstitutional, 47–48; with private sector, 52–53; at state and regional levels, 50–52; and team teaching, 49–50
Technology costs, 41–61; of distance learning environments, 57–58; and economic life cycle, 56–57; infrastructure servicing and, 54; mandatory student fees and, 58–59; price and, 53; student ownership/leasing and, 59–61; support services and, 54–55; tangible versus intangible, 57–58. *See also* Fiscal planning
Technology interfaces, standardization of, 82–83
Technology leadership, 44
Technology quality, 63–85, 93–94; accreditation and, 63–64; Internet content and, 64–65, 67–70
Teller, E., 87–88
Textbook publishers, academic alliances with, 52
"Three Definitions of Critical Thinking," 16
Tillman, H. N., 65, 66, 70
Trevitt, C., 73
Trow, M., 21
Twigg, C., 7, 9, 10, 47
Tyack, D., 2, 11–12, 68

U

Universal Service, 33
Updegrove, D., 41, 54

V

Vasquez, L., 37
Very High Performance Backbone Network Service (vBNS), 70
Virtual university. *See* Distance education
Vision, institutional, 46–47

W

Wack, M., 93
Waggoner, M. D., 81
Wagner, E. D., 2, 3, 71
Wendel, F. C., 47, 50
"When Students Have Learning Disabilities," 39
Wiggins, G., 78, 79
Wight, J. D., 30
Williams, R., 73
Willis, D. J., 82
Wills, S., 77
Winn, W., 99
Winston, G., 90
Wolfe, A., 1, 91
World Wide Web, 64; instruction based on, 58; as research instrument, 65–66

Y

Young, J. R., 47, 59

Z

Zemsky, R., 45–46
Ziegahn, L., 71

The mission of the Educational Resources Information Center (ERIC) system is to improve American education by increasing and facilitating the use of educational research and information on practice in the activities of learning, teaching, educational decision making, and research, wherever and whenever these activities take place.

Since 1983, the ASHE-ERIC Higher Education Report Series has been published in cooperation with the Association for the Study of Higher Education (ASHE). Starting in 2000, the series is published by Jossey-Bass in conjunction with the ERIC Clearinghouse on Higher Education.

Each monograph is the definitive analysis of a tough higher education problem, based on thorough research of pertinent literature and institutional experiences. Topics are identified by a national survey. Noted practitioners and scholars are then commissioned to write the reports, with experts providing critical reviews of each manuscript before publication.

Eight monographs (10 before 1985) in the ASHE-ERIC Higher Education Report series are published each year and are available on individual and subscription bases. To order, use the order form on the last page of this book.

Qualified persons interested in writing a monograph for the ASHE-ERIC Higher Education Report series are invited to submit a proposal to the National Advisory Board. As the preeminent literature review and issue analysis series in higher education, the Higher Education Reports are guaranteed wide dissemination and national exposure for accepted candidates. Execution of a monograph requires at least a minimal familiarity with the ERIC database, including *Resources in Education* and the current *Index to Journals in Education*. The objective of these reports is to bridge conventional wisdom with practical research.

ADVISORY BOARD

Susan Frost
Office of Institutional Planning and Research
Emory University

Kenneth Feldman
SUNY at Stony Brook

Anna Ortiz
Michigan State University

James Fairweather
Michigan State University

Lori White
Stanford University

Esther E. Gottlieb
West Virginia University

Carol Colbeck
Pennsylvania State University

Jeni Hart
University of Arizona

CONSULTING EDITORS

Steven Sachs
Northern Virginia Community College

Jacques DuBois
Synergy Plus, Inc.

Diana Oblinger
International Business Machines Corporation

Kenneth C. Green
The Campus Computing Project

Scott Swail
The College Board

REVIEW PANEL

Kassie Freeman
Peabody College

Philo A. Hutcheson
Georgia State University

Timothy Gallineau
Buffalo State College

Elizabeth A. Jones
West Virginia University

Toby Milton
Essex Community College

William Tierney
University of Southern California

Susan B. Twombly
University of Kansas

RECENT TITLES

Volume 27 ASHE-ERIC Higher Education Reports

1. The Art and Science of Classroom Assessment: The Missing Part of Pedagogy
   Susan M. Brookhart

2. Due Process and Higher Education: A Systemic Approach to Fair Decision Making
   Ed Stevens

3. Grading Students' Classroom Writing: Issues and Strategies
   Bruce W. Speck

4. Posttenure Faculty Development: Building a System for Faculty Improvement and Appreciation
   Jeffrey W. Alstete

Volume 26 ASHE-ERIC Higher Education Reports

1. Faculty Workload Studies: Perspectives, Needs, and Future Directions
   Katrina A. Meyer

2. Assessing Faculty Publication Productivity: Issues of Equity
   Elizabeth G. Creamer

3. Proclaiming and Sustaining Excellence: Assessment as a Faculty Role
   Karen Maitland Schilling and Karl L. Schilling

4. Creating Learning Centered Classrooms: What Does Learning Theory Have to Say?
   Frances K. Stage, Patricia A. Muller, Jillian Kinzie, and Ada Simmons

5. The Academic Administrator and the Law: What Every Dean and Department Chair Needs to Know
   J. Douglas Toma and Richard L. Palm

6. The Powerful Potential of Learning Communities: Improving Education for the Future
   Oscar T. Lenning and Larry H. Ebbers

7. Enrollment Management for the 21st Century: Institutional Goals, Accountability, and Fiscal Responsibility
   Garlene Penn

8. Enacting Diverse Learning Environments: Improving the Climate for Racial/Ethnic Diversity in Higher Education
   Sylvia Hurtado, Jeffrey Milem, Alma Clayton-Pedersen, and Walter Allen

Volume 25 ASHE-ERIC Higher Education Reports

1. A Culture for Academic Excellence: Implementing the Quality Principles in Higher Education
   Jann E. Freed, Marie R. Klugman, and Jonathan D. Fife

Volume 23 ASHE-ERIC Higher Education Reports

1. The Advisory Committee Advantage: Creating an Effective Strategy for Programmatic Improvement
   Lee Teitel

2. Collaborative Peer Review: The Role of Faculty in Improving College Teaching
   Larry Keig and Michael D. Waggoner

3. Prices, Productivity, and Investment: Assessing Financial Strategies in Higher Education
   Edward P. St. John

4. The Development Officer in Higher Education: Toward an Understanding of the Role
   Michael J. Worth and James W. Asp II

5. Measuring Up: The Promises and Pitfalls of Performance Indicators in Higher Education
   Gerald Gaither, Brian P. Nedwek, and John E. Neal

6. A New Alliance: Continuous Quality and Classroom Effectiveness
   Mimi Wolverton

7. Redesigning Higher Education: Producing Dramatic Gains in Student Learning
   Lion F. Gardiner

8. Student Learning Outside the Classroom: Transcending Artificial Boundaries
   George D. Kuh, Katie Branch Douglas, Jon P. Lund, and Jackie Ramin-Gyurnek

Back Issue/Subscription Order Form

Copy or detach and send to:

Jossey-Bass Inc., Publishers, 350 Sansome Street, San Francisco CA 94104-1342

Call or fax toll free!

Phone 888-378-2537 6AM-5PM PST; Fax 800-605-2665

Individual reports: Please send me the following reports at $24 each

(Important: please include series initials and issue number, such as AEHE 27:1)

1. AEHE _____

_____

_____

$ _____ Total for individual reports

$ _____ Shipping charges (for individual reports *only;* subscriptions are exempt from shipping charges): Up to $30, add $5^{50} • $30^{01}–$50, add $6^{50} $50^{01}–$75, add $8 • $75^{01}–$100, add $10 • $100^{01}–$150, add $12 Over $150, call for shipping charge

Subscriptions Please ❑ start ❑ renew my subscription to *ASHE-ERIC Higher Education Reports* for the year 2000 at the following rate (8 issues): U.S. $144 Canada: $169 All others: $174

Please ❑ start my subscription to *ASHE-ERIC Higher Education Reports* for the year 2001 at the following rate (8 issues): U.S. $108 Canada: $133 All others: $138

NOTE: Subscriptions are for the calendar year only. Subscriptions begin with Report 1 of the year indicated above.

$ _____ Total individual reports and subscriptions (Add appropriate sales tax for your state for individual reports. No sales tax on U.S. subscriptions. Canadian residents, add GST for subscriptions and individual reports.)

❑ Payment enclosed (U.S. check or money order only)

❑ VISA, MC, AmEx, Discover Card # Exp. date

Signature _____ Day phone _____

❑ Bill me (U.S. institutional orders only. Purchase order required)

Purchase order #_____

Federal Tax ID 1355   GST 89102-8052

Name _____

Address _____

_____

Phone_____ E-mail _____

For more information about Jossey-Bass Publishers, visit our Web site at: www.josseybass.com   **PRIORITY CODE = ND1**